Thirty Years of Learning Environments

Advances in Learning Environments Research

Series Editors

Barry J. Fraser (*Curtin University of Technology, Australia*)
David B. Zandvliet (*Simon Fraser University, Canada*)

Editorial Board

Perry den Brok (*Eindhoven University of Technology, The Netherlands*)
Shwu-yong Huang (*National Taiwan University, Taiwan*)
Bruce Johnson (*University of Arizona, USA*)
Celia Johnson (*Bradley University, USA*)
Rosalyn Anstine Templeton (*Montana State University-Northern, USA*)

VOLUME 11

The titles published in this series are listed at *brill.com/aler*

Thirty Years of Learning Environments

Looking Back and Looking Forward

Edited by

David B. Zandvliet
Barry J. Fraser

BRILL
SENSE

LEIDEN | BOSTON

All chapters in this book have undergone peer review.

The Library of Congress Cataloging-in-Publication Data is available online at http://catalog.loc.gov

Typeface for the Latin, Greek, and Cyrillic scripts: "Brill". See and download: brill.com/brill-typeface.

ISSN 2542-9035
ISBN 978-90-04-38769-0 (paperback)
ISBN 978-90-04-38770-6 (hardback)
ISBN 978-90-04-38772-0 (e-book)

Copyright 2019 by Koninklijke Brill NV, Leiden, The Netherlands.
Koninklijke Brill NV incorporates the imprints Brill, Brill Hes & De Graaf, Brill Nijhoff, Brill Rodopi, Brill Sense, Hotei Publishing, mentis Verlag, Verlag Ferdinand Schöningh and Wilhelm Fink Verlag.
All rights reserved. No part of this publication may be reproduced, translated, stored in a retrieval system, or transmitted in any form or by any means, electronic, mechanical, photocopying, recording or otherwise, without prior written permission from the publisher.
Authorization to photocopy items for internal or personal use is granted by Koninklijke Brill NV provided that the appropriate fees are paid directly to The Copyright Clearance Center, 222 Rosewood Drive, Suite 910, Danvers, MA 01923, USA. Fees are subject to change.

This book is printed on acid-free paper and produced in a sustainable manner.

Contents

List of Figures and Tables   VII

1   Milestones in the Evolution of the Learning Environments Field over the Past Three Decades   1
     Barry J. Fraser

2   My Journey in the Learning Environments Research Community
     Research on Teacher–Student Interactions and Relationships   20
     Theo Wubbels

3   Developments in Quantitative Methods and Analyses for Studying Learning Environments   41
     Perry den Brok, Tim Mainhard and Theo Wubbels

4   Looking Back and Looking Forward   59
     David B. Zandvliet

5   Evaluating the Impact of a Purposefully-Designed Active Learning Space on Student Outcomes and Behaviours in an Undergraduate Architecture Course   72
     Catherine Martin-Dunlop, Christine Hohmann, Mary Anne Alabanza Akers, Jim Determan, LaKeisha Lewter and Isaac Williams

6   Development and Validation of the Questionnaire Assessing Connections to Science (QuACS)   102
     Georgeos Sirrakos, Jr. and Barry J. Fraser

7   Using Classroom Environment Perceptions to Guide Teacher Professional Learning
     A Mixed-Methods Case Study   127
     David Henderson and Melissa Loh

8   Impacts of Learning Environments on Student Well-Being in Higher Education   141
     Alisa Stanton, David B. Zandvliet and Rosie Dhaliwal

Figures and Tables

Figures

2.1 The Inter Personal Circle for the Teacher (IPC). 23
2.2 Interpersonal circle for students. 29
2.3 Example of time series measurement every 0.5 seconds of teacher and students for communion and agency (dotted line represents students and continuous line represents the teacher). 30
4.1 Ecological factors contributing to learning environments. 63
5.1 Racial/ethnic composition of undergraduate architecture students who participated in the study (N=49). 79
5.2 Average item means for four variables in Moos' system maintenance and change dimension comparing architecture students' perceptions in the control (traditional) group (n_1 = 22) and in the experimental (enriched, active learning) group (n_2 = 19). 86
5.3 Average item means of four variables in Moos' personal development dimension comparing architecture students' perceptions in the control (traditional) group (n_1 = 22) and in the experimental (enriched, active learning) group (n_2 = 19). 87
5.4 Average item means of four variables in Moos' relationship dimension comparing architecture students' perceptions in the control (traditional) group (n_1 = 22) and in the experimental (enriched, active learning) group (n_2 = 19). 87
5.5 Results of coding five types of behaviour – movement, student-to-student interaction, student-to-instructor interaction, interaction with the physical environment, and disengagement – that students engaged in during the course, design and human behaviour, spring and fall semesters of 2014 (N = 49). 88
5.6 Photograph of experimental/active learning classroom showing smaller, mobile whiteboards, monitors near each group, round tables and chairs on casters. 90
5.7 Photograph of architecture students and the instructor (third from right) in the experimental/active learning classroom involved in a discussion. 91
7.1 Example of pretest feedback to teachers regarding students' perceptions of actual and preferred learning environment. 131
7.2 Extract from pretest report showing items means for teacher support scale. 132
7.3 Example of pretest and posttest feedback to teachers regarding students' perceptions of actual and preferred learning environment. 132

Tables

1.1   Selected findings from 21 studies using the WIHIC.   6
5.1   Overview of scales (in italics) from four instruments used to create the architecture learning environment survey (ALES).   83
5.2   Scales and items from the architecture learning environment survey (ALES) that specifically assess the physical features of a learning space.   84
5.3   Comparison of average class grade, average GPA, and ratio between class grade divided by overall GPA for architecture students in the control and experimental groups (N = 45).   89
6.1   Preliminary structure of the questionnaire assessing connections to science (QuACS).   111
6.2   Factor analysis results for learning environment scales.   113
6.3   Factor analysis results for attitude scales.   114
6.4   Final structure of the questionnaire assessing connections to science.   116
7.1   CCQ scales and their allocation to three dimensions.   130
8.1   Descriptive statistics for the life satisfaction variable for three learning environment groups.   145
8.2   ANOVA results for differences among three learning environment groups in ratings of life satisfaction.   146
8.3   Games-Howell post hoc test for multiple comparisons of life satisfaction across three learning environment groupings.   146

CHAPTER 1

Milestones in the Evolution of the Learning Environments Field over the Past Three Decades

Barry J. Fraser
Curtin University, Perth, Australia

An influential milestone in the history of the field of learning environments occurred during the 1984 annual meeting of the American Educational Research Association (AERA) in New Orleans. Chad Ellett, Herbert Walberg and I decided to form an AERA Special Interest Group (SIG) originally called The Study of Learning Environments but now simply named SIG Learning Environments. A successful application to AERA led to the SIG being allocated its first program space at the AERA annual meeting in Chicago in 1985.

Since 1985, the field of learning environments has continued to grow in both its size and international reach until, by the time of the SIG's 30th anniversary in 2015, the AERA annual meeting (also held in Chicago) had 105 presentations listed in its index under the term 'learning environments'. This current book is a celebration and record of progress in the field of learning environments during the SIG's first 30 years.

In his chapter in this book, Wubbels evaluates the contribution of the SIG Learning Environments in ways that would resonate with many SIG members. He considers that the SIG has been "an inspiring event in (his) professional and personal life", was of "the utmost importance in developing the program of research of (his) research group" and has "helped (him) to build a network with researchers from other countries because of the strong international character of the SIG". He also noted that, during his first AERA annual meeting, he "felt like a stranger in a new world, running all day from session to session"; the SIG has proved to be a home for many of us and reduced some of this rushing around. Wubbels also noted that the SIG has advanced both the field of learning environments and its members' careers by providing an annual best paper award and an opportunity to publish research initially in the SIG's annual monograph and now in the journal described below.

Following the formation of the AERA SIG Learning Environment in 1985, another important landmark in 1998 was the birth of *Learning Environments Research: An International Journal* (LERI) first published by Kluwer, then Springer and now Springer Nature. In keeping with the international character of research on learning environments, LERI has a European Editor (initially Theo Wubbels and now Perry den Brok), a North American Editor (initially Ken Tobin and now Hersch Waxman) and an Australasian Editor (initially Darrell Fisher and now Jill Aldridge) in addition to an Editor-in-Chief (Barry Fraser). LERI has now completed 20 successful years and is ranked in Quadrant 1 of Scimago for one or more disciplines.

After another 10 years, a book series was initiated entitled *Advances in Research on Learning Environments* and published by Sense Publishers (now Brill Sense). The original co-editors were Barry Fraser and Jeff Dorman, but today David Zandvliet has taken over from Jeff Dorman. This book series now has completed 10 successful years.

1   Introduction

It was noted by Fraser (2001) that, because students spend approximately 20,000 hours in classrooms by the time they graduate from university, learning–teaching experiences and student–teacher interactions are just as important as students' achievement outcomes. What the past 30 years of learning environment research has convincingly established is that the subtle construct of learning environment can be reliably and validly measured (typically through the eyes of the participants themselves) and that attention to creating positive classroom environments is likely to pay off in terms of improving student outcomes.

The birth of the field learning environments often is attributed to the simultaneous but independent programs of research of Herbert Walberg and Rudolf Moos. Walberg developed the Learning Environment Inventory (LEI) as part of the research and evaluation of Harvard Project Physics (Walberg & Anderson, 1968) and Moos' work with the Classroom Environment Scale (CES) was part of an extensive research program on nine different human environments (including hospitals, prisons and work milieus) (Moos, 1974; Moos & Trickett, 1974).

An influential antecedent to Walberg's and Moos' work in educational settings was Lewin's (1936) field theory in business settings. Lewin's formula, $B = f(P, E)$, stressed the need to consider behaviour as a function of both the person and the environment. This model was modified and expanded by Walberg (1970) to become $L = f(I, A, E)$, with learning being a function of instructional, attitudinal and environmental characteristics.

An enduring contribution to the field of educational environments is Moos' (1974) scheme for classifying all human environments (including education) according to three basic types of dimensions. *Relationship* dimensions identify the nature and intensity of personal relationships within the environment and assess the extent to which people are involved in the environment and support and help each other. *Personal Development* dimensions assess basic directions along which personal growth and self-enhancement occur. *System Maintenance and System Change* dimensions involve the extent to which the environment is orderly, clear in expectations, maintains control and is responsive to change. Today, researchers still continue to classify the scales in their learning environment questionnaires into Moos three general dimensions.

Prior to the birth of SIG Learning Environments in 1985, there were several noteworthy research efforts that grew out of and built upon the pioneering foundations laid in the USA by Walberg with the Learning Environment Inventory and Moos with the Classroom Environment Scale. Because both the LEI and CES were designed for use in teacher-centred classrooms, the Individualised Classroom Environment Questionnaire (ICEQ) was created in Australia to assess those dimensions that are salient in student-centred classrooms (Rentoul & Fraser, 1979). The ICEQ's dimensions are Personalisation, Participation, Independence, Investigation and Differentiation. The ICEQ was used to establish associations with students' attitudes to science (Fraser & Butts, 1982; Fraser & Fisher, 1982), that actual-preferred congruence (i.e. person–environment fit) could be as important as individualisation per se (Fraser & Fisher, 1983). Although the ICEQ eventually was made available by a test publisher (Fraser, 1990), its take-up and use were somewhat limited, although several of the ICEQ's dimensions have been incorporated into later learning environment instruments.

A simplified version of the LEI, called the My Class Inventory (MCI), was developed by the original LEI's authors for use with primary-school students. This original version of the MCI was simplified by Fisher and Fraser (1981) and then modified to form a highly-convenient 25-item short form (Fraser & O'Brien, 1985). Because of its unusually low reading level, researchers have continued to use the MCI over the ensuing decades (Goh & Fraser, 1998; Majeed, Fraser, & Aldridge, 2002; Scott Houston, Fraser, & Ledbetter, 2008; Sink & Spencer, 2005).

Because the LEI and CES were developed for use at the secondary-school level, the College and University Classroom Environment Inventory (CUCEI) was developed to assess somewhat similar dimensions at the higher-education level (Fraser & Treagust, 1986; Fraser, Treagust, & Dennis, 1986). Some noteworthy applications of the CUCEI include an evaluation of alternative senior-high schools (Fraser, Williamson, & Tobin, 1987), assessment of the learning environment of computer classroom environments (Logan, Crump, & Rennie, 2006), an investigation of how inverted/flipped classrooms influence the learning environment (Strayer, 2012) and an evaluation of teaching strategies for adults who experienced childhood difficulties in learning mathematics (Hasan & Fraser, 2015).

The years leading up to the formation of the SIG in 1985 witnessed the birth in the Netherlands of one of the largest and most significant programs of learning environment research. This program is described in Wubbels' chapter in this book and in Wubbels and Brekelmans (2012). This research introduced a model of interpersonal behaviour based on Leary (1957) and involved use of the Questionnaire on Teacher Interaction (QTI) in the Dutch language. Interestingly, the SIG provided the impetus to translate the QTI into English, which was a catalyst for the expansion and uptake of this research program in many countries around the world.

The next two sections are devoted to, respectively, questionnaires for assessing the learning environment and research applications with learning environment assessments.

2 Questionnaires for Assessing Learning Environments

> A historical look at the field of learning environment … shows that a striking feature is the availability of a variety of economical, valid and widely-applicable questionnaires that have been developed and used for assessing students' perceptions of classroom environment. Few fields in education can boast the existence of such a rich array of validated and robust instruments which have been used in so many research applications. (Fraser, 1988, pp. 7–8)

Already in this chapter, brief mention has been made of two pioneering learning environment questionnaires, namely, Walberg's Learning Environment Inventory (LEI) and Moos' Classroom Environment Scale (CES), that marked the birth of research specifically on educational environments. Also, the remarkable program of research that Wubbels initiated in the Netherlands using the Questionnaire on Teacher Interaction (QTI) has been quickly introduced (see Goh & Fraser, 2000). As well, some of the earlier questionnaires developed by Fraser in Australia were mentioned: the Individualised Classroom Environment Questionnaire (ICEQ) and College and University Classroom Environment Inventory (CUCEI). The application of these questionnaires has been facilitated by the availability of preferred forms (Byrne, Hattie, & Fraser, 1986), as well as actual forms, and of economical short forms (Fraser & Fisher, 1983).

Below an introduction is provided to the Science Laboratory Environment Inventory (SLEI), Constructivist Learning Environment Survey (CLES) and the What Is Happening In this Class? (WIHIC), as well as some other questionnaires that include many of the WIHIC's scales.

2.1 Science Laboratory Environment Inventory (SLEI)

A unique and important setting in science education is the science laboratory classroom. The Science Laboratory Environment Inventory (SLEI) was developed to assess the unique dimensions that characterise science laboratory classes (Fraser, Giddings, & McRobbie, 1995; Fraser & McRobbie, 1995). This 35-item questionnaire has five scales (Student Cohesiveness, Open-Endedness, Integration, Rule Clarity and Material Environment) and a five-point frequency response scale (Almost Never, Seldom, Sometimes, Often and Very Often). It is noteworthy that the SLEI was field tested and validated simultaneously in six countries (USA, England, Canada, Australia, Israel and Nigeria) with a large sample of 5447 students in 269 classes (Fraser, Giddings, & McRobbie, 1995). Subsequently, the SLEI has been used in research in chemistry classes in Singapore (Wong & Fraser, 1996), high-school science classes in Korea (Fraser & Lee, 2009), high-school biology classes in the USA (Lightburn & Fraser, 2007) and middle-school science classes in Australia (Rogers & Fraser, 2013).

2.2 Constructivist Learning Environment Survey (CLES)

Taylor, Fraser, and Fisher (1997) developed the Constructivist Learning Environment Survey (CLES) for assessing the extent to which a classroom's environment is consistent with constructivism. Its 35 items in five scales (Personal Relevance, Uncertainty, Critical Voice, Shared Control and Student Negotiation) are responded to using a five-point frequency scale. The CLES has been cross-validated and found to be useful in research applications in numerous countries, including: a cross-cultural study of lower-secondary science classrooms in Taiwan (n = 1879) and Australia (n = 1081) (Aldridge, Fraser, Taylor, & Chen, 2000); 1864 grade 4–6 mathematics students in South Africa (Aldridge, Fraser, & Sebela, 2004); 1079 science students whose teachers in Texas underwent professional development (Nix, Fraser, & Ledbetter, 2005); 3207 secondary-school business studies students in Singapore (Koh & Fraser, 2014); and 739 grade K–3 science students in Florida who responded to a modified version of the CLES in English or Spanish (Peiro & Fraser, 2009).

2.3 What Is Happening in This Class? (WIHIC)

It was noted by Dorman (2008) that the What Is Happening In this Class? (WIHIC) questionnaire is used so frequently around the world that it has achieved "almost bandwagon status" (p. 181). Its 56 items fall into seven scales (Student Cohesiveness, Teacher Support, Involvement, Investigation, Task Orientation, Cooperation and Equity).

To illustrate the WIHIC's wide usage for many purposes around the world, Table 1.1 has been assembled to include 21 studies that employed the WIHIC

TABLE 1.1 Selected findings from 21 studies using the WIHIC

Location	References	Sample	Selected findings
Taiwan & Australia	Aldridge and Fraser (2000); Aldridge, Fraser, and Huang (1999)	1879 Taiwanese & 1081 Australian junior-high science students	Validated WIHIC in two languages. Learning environment differences between Taiwan & Australia.
Indonesia & Australia	Fraser, Aldridge, and Adolphe (2010)	594 Indonesian and 567 Australian secondary science students	Cross-validated WIHIC in two languages. Differences between countries and sexes.
Singapore	Lim and Fraser (in press)	441 grade 6 English students	WIHIC was cross-validated. Classroom environment varied with student sex and ethnicity.
Singapore	Chionh and Fraser (2009)	2310 grade 10 geography & mathematics students	Validated WIHIC for two school subjects. Differences between school subjects.
Singapore	Goh and Fraser (2016)	485 grade 6 science students	WIHIC was cross-validated. Differences between sexes and between actual and preferred environments.
Jordan	Alzubaidi, Aldridge, and Khine (2016)	994 university students of English as a second language	Arabic version of WIHIC was validated. Learning environment related to student motivation and self-regulation.

TABLE 1.1 Selected findings from 21 studies using the WIHIC (cont.)

Location	References	Sample	Selected findings
China	Bi (2015)	1235 grade 7–11 English students	Modified WIHIC was validated. Small sex differences in learning environment perceptions. Weak relationships between classroom environment and oral English.
China	Liu and Fraser (2013)	945 English majors aged 18–20 years	Several WIHIC scales related to English language motivation.
Korea	Baek and Choi (2002)	1012 grade 11 & 12 English students	WIHIC scores varied with school and classroom organisation and correlated with English achievement.
Korea	Kim, Fisher, and Fraser (2000)	543 grade 8 science students	Korean WIHIC was validated. Sex differences in learning environment perceptions.
South Africa	Aldridge, Fraser, and Ntuli (2009)	1077 grade 4–7 students	Validated WIHIC in IsiZulu language. Preservice teachers in a distance-education program used environment perceptions to improve classroom environments.
UAE	Afari, Aldridge, Fraser, and Khine (2013)	352 college mathematics students	Arabic WIHIC was validated. Using mathematics games promoted positive classroom environments. Females perceived environments more favourably.

TABLE 1.1 Selected findings from 21 studies using the WIHIC (*cont.*)

Location	References	Sample	Selected findings
Myanmar	Khine et al. (2018)	251 first-year university science students	Validated Myanmar version of WIHIC. No sex differences in correlations between WIHIC scales.
India	Koul and Fisher (2005)	1021 science students	Cross-validated WIHIC. Learning environment differences between cultural backgrounds.
Greece	Charalampous and Kokkinos (2017)	Groups of 504 and 984 elementary students	Validated a modified Greek language version of WIHIC (G-EWIHIC) for elementary students.
USA	Cohn and Fraser (2016)	1097 grade 7 & 8 science students in New York	Cross-validated WIHIC. Large learning environment differences between users and non-users of Student Response Systems.
USA	Wolf and Fraser (2008)	1434 middle-school science students in New York	Inquiry laboratory activities had more favourable learning environments on some dimensions.
USA	Martin-Dunlop and Fraser (2008)	525 female university science students in California	Large increases in learning environment scores for an innovative course.
USA	Skordi and Fraser (in press)	375 university business statistics students in California	Validated WIHIC for use in university statistics classes. Sex differences in WIHIC scores. Relationship between some WIHIC scales and student achievement and enjoyment.

MILESTONES IN THE EVOLUTION OF THE LEARNING ENVIRONMENTS 9

TABLE 1.1 Selected findings from 21 studies using the WIHIC (*cont.*)

Location	References	Sample	Selected findings
USA	Helding and Fraser (2013)	924 grades 8 &10 science students in Florida	Validated WIHIC in English and Spanish. Students of teachers with National Board Certification perceived more favourable learning environments.
USA	Zaragoza and Fraser (2017)	765 grade 5 science students from Florida	Validated a modified version of WIHIC in field-study classrooms. Field-study classes had much more positive environments than traditional classes, especially for students with limited English proficiency.

in 13 countries and in 12 languages. The studies in this table not only provide comprehensive cross-validation for the WIHIC in its original, modified and/or translated form, but capture some of the major applications and findings from this body of research with the WIHIC.

2.4 Inclusion of WIHIC Scales in Other Learning Environment Questionnaires

Many or all WIHIC scales have been chosen for inclusion in later specific-purpose learning environment questionnaires. For example, in order to monitor the implementation of outcomes-based education and in South Africa, Aldridge, Laugksch, Seopa, and Fraser (2006) included scales from the WIHIC in the Outcomes-Based Learning Environment Questionnaire (OBLEQ). In research into the evolution of the learning environment in an innovative new senior-high school, the Technology-Rich Outcomes-Focused Learning Environment Inventory (TROFLEI) was developed to include all seven WIHIC scales together with the scales of Differentiation, Computer Usage, and Young Adult Ethos (Aldridge, Dorman, & Fraser, 2004; Aldridge & Fraser, 2008; Dorman & Fraser, 2009).

The Constructivist-Oriented Learning Environment Scale (COLES) provides feedback from students for teachers to use in improving learning environments (Bell & Aldridge, 2014; Aldridge, Fraser, Bell, & Dorman, 2012). The COLES includes all of the WIHIC's scales except Investigation and also includes Differentiation from the ICEQ, Personal Relevance from the CLES, Young Adult Ethos from the TROFLEI and, significantly, two new scales related to assessment (namely, Formative Assessment and Assessment Criteria). The COLES was validated with 2043 grades 11 and 12 students in 147 classes in Australia (Aldridge et al., 2012).

In the Greek language, the How Chemistry Class is Working (HCCW) questionnaire includes selected WIHIC scales and it was used to identify differences between Greek and Cypriot students in their classroom environment perceptions (Giallousi, Gialamas, Spyrellis, & Plavlatou, 2010). More recently in Greece, Charalampous and Kokkinos (2017) reported a particularly thorough attempt to develop and validate a new elementary-school version of the WIHIC in the Greek language; this version is known as the G-EWIHIC.

3 Some Research Applications

Fraser (2012, 2014) has identified numerous applications of learning environment assessments, including in the work of school psychologists (e.g. Burden

& Fraser, 1993), as criteria of effectiveness in the evaluation of educational programs, innovations and provisions (e.g. Spinner & Fraser, 2005), associations between the classroom environment and students' cognitive and effective outcomes (e.g. see reviews of Fraser, 2012, 2014) and as feedback in teachers' action research attempts to change their classrooms (e.g. Fraser & Aldridge, 2017). Some of these applications are considered in more detail below.

In the insightful and useful chapter by den Brok, Mainhard and Wubbels in the current book, some of the developments in methods for the statistical analysis of learning environment data are identified. Some noteworthy examples include hierarchical linear modelling (HLM), structural equation modelling (SEM), Rasch modelling and confirmatory factor analysis. (It is noteworthy that, at the time of the development and validation of Walberg's historic Learning Environment Inventory and Moos' historic Classroom Environment Scale, not even exploratory factor analysis was readily available and used.)

3.1   Evaluation of Educational Programs

Walberg's historic evaluation of Harvard Project Physics revealed that the new and the traditional physics curriculum could be distinguished in terms of students' classroom environment perceptions (using the Learning Environment Inventory) when a range of student outcome measures showed little differentiation (Welch & Walberg, 1972). Over the ensuing decades, learning environment dimensions have continued to prove useful criteria of effectiveness in evaluating teacher professional development (Nix, Fraser, & Ledbetter, 2005), field study centres (Zaragoza & Fraser, 2017), National Board certification of teachers (Helding & Fraser, 2013), inclusion of games in mathematics teaching (Afari, Aldridge, Fraser, & Khine, 2013), computer-assisted learning (Teh & Fraser, 1995), use of reality pedagogy in science teaching (Sirrakos & Fraser, 2017) and the implementation of student response systems (Cohn & Fraser, 2016).

3.2   Improving Classroom Environments

In 1981, Fraser proposed a simple five-step model for teachers to use in their attempts to improve their classroom environments by utilising feedback from students about their perceptions on questionnaires assessing classroom learning environment (Fraser, 1981). In 2017, Fraser and Aldridge reviewed the intermittent application of this approach during the ensuing decades and its evolution into more sophisticated methods for scoring questionnaires and graphically depicting feedback (Fraser & Aldridge, 2017). For example, in South Africa, Aldridge, Fraser, and Sebela (2004) reported how teachers used the

CLES with 1864 grade 4–9 students in attempts to improve their classrooms. In Australia, Aldridge, Fraser, Bell, and Dorman (2012) reported teachers' use of the 11 scales from the COLES in successful attempts to improve classroom environments.

Aldridge and Fraser (2008) reported some case studies of how teachers at a new senior-high school used the TROFLEI in attempts to improve their classroom environments, while Fraser and Aldridge (2017) reported a detailed case study of one teacher's attempt to improve her classroom environment using the COLES. In their chapter in this book, Henderson and Loh report the use of students' learning environment perceptions on the COLES to guide teachers' professional learning at one school. This mixed-method study, which involved about 25 teachers and 500 students each year, revealed just how highly teachers valued this kind of feedback in supporting their professional learning. A recent whole-school principal-led attempt at improving a school's classroom environments involved 2673 grade 8–12 students and 171 teachers (Rijken, Fraser, & Aldridge, 2016) and revealed statistically-significant improvements in both the learning environment and students' self-efficacy.

3.3 *Physical Learning Environments*

Recently, attention to psychosocial characteristics of learning environments has been supplemented by interest in the physical environment of educational buildings and learning spaces. This trend is reflected in the chapter in this volume by Martin-Dunlop and colleagues and in several books in Brill Sense's *Advances in Learning Environments Research* series (Alterator & Deed, 2018; Fisher, 2016, in press; Imms, Cleveland & Fisher, 2016) and in various articles (e.g. Cleveland & Fisher, 2013). In the chapter by Martin-Dunlop's transdisciplinary team in the current book, the impact of an enriched and active learning space for university architecture students was evaluated using questionnaire surveys, lesson videotapes, interviews and achievement data.

Although new designs or redesigns for learning-teaching spaces often aim to transform the psychosocial learning environment in specific ways, it is rare for researchers to evaluate their effectiveness in terms of changes in psychosocial characteristics. For example, Prain (2018) reported that 2500 students' perceptions of personalised learning did not improve over three years in new schools which aimed to promote personalised learning. Therefore, Skordi and Fraser (in press) attempted to show how methods, conceptual frameworks and research traditions from the field of learning environment can potentially be applied in evaluating the success of changes in educational spaces in promoting positive changes in psychosocial and pedagogical characteristics of learning environments.

4 Conclusion

This chapter has identified some of the significant milestones in the expansion and internationalisation of the field of learning environments research over the past three decades since the formation of the AERA SIG Learning Environments in 1985. As this book demonstrates, the learning environment field currently is ripe for further exciting new developments in future decades.

References

Afari, E., Aldridge, J. M., Fraser, B. J., & Khine, M. S. (2013). Students' perceptions of the learning environment and attitudes in game-based mathematics classrooms. *Learning Environments Research, 16*, 131–150.

Aldridge, J. M., Dorman, J. P., & Fraser, B. J. (2004). Use of multitrait-multimethod modelling to validate actual and preferred forms of the Technology-Rich Outcomes-Focused Learning Environment Inventory (TROFLEI). *Australian Journal of Educational and Developmental Psychology, 4*, 110–125.

Aldridge, J. M., & Fraser, B. J. (2000). A cross-cultural study of classroom learning environments in Australia and Taiwan. *Learning Environments Research, 3*, 101–134.

Aldridge, J. M., & Fraser, B. J. (2008). *Outcomes-focused learning environments: Determinants and effects* (Advances in Learning Environments Research Series). Rotterdam, The Netherlands: Sense Publishers.

Aldridge, J. M., Fraser, B. J., Bell, L., & Dorman, J. P. (2012). Using a new learning environment questionnaire for reflection in teacher action research. *Journal of Science Teacher Education, 23*, 259–290.

Aldridge, J. M., Fraser, B. J., & Huang, I. T.-C. (1999). Investigating classroom environments in Taiwan and Australia with multiple research methods. *Journal of Educational Research, 93*, 48–62.

Aldridge, J. M., Fraser, B. J., & Ntuli, S. (2009). Utilising learning environment assessments to improve teaching practices among in-service teachers undertaking a distance education programme. *South African Journal of Education, 29*, 147–170.

Aldridge, J. M., Fraser, B. J., & Sebela, M. P. (2004). Using teacher action research to promote constructivist learning environments in South Africa. *South African Journal of Education, 24*, 245–253.

Aldridge, J. M., Fraser, B. J., Taylor, P. C., & Chen, C.-C. (2000). Constructivist learning environments in a cross-national study in Taiwan and Australia. *International Journal of Science Education, 22*, 37–55.

Aldridge, J. M., Laugksch, R. C., Seopa, M. A., & Fraser, B. J. (2006). Development and validation of an instrument to monitor the implementation of outcomes-based learning environments in science classrooms in South Africa. *International Journal of Science Education, 28*, 45–70.

Alterator, S., & Deed, C. (Eds.). (2018). *School space and its occupation: Conceptualising and evaluating innovative learning environments* (Advances in Learning Environments Research Series). Leiden, The Netherlands: Brill Sense.

Alzubaidi, E., Aldridge, J. M., & Khine, M. S. (2016). Learning English as a second language at the university level in Jordan: Motivation, self-regulation and learning environment perceptions. *Learning Environments Research, 19*(1), 133–152.

Baek, S. G., & Choi, H. J. (2002). The relationship between students' perceptions of classroom environment and their academic achievement in Korea. *Asia-Pacific Journal of Education, 3*(1), 125–135.

Bell, L. M., & Aldridge, J. M. (2014). *Student voice, teacher action research and classroom improvement* (Advances in Learning Environments Research Series). Rotterdam, The Netherlands: Sense Publishers.

Bi, X. (2015). Associations between psychosocial aspects of English classroom environments and motivation types of Chinese tertiary-level English majors. *Learning Environments Research, 18*(1), 95–110.

Burden, R. L., & Fraser, B. J. (1993). Use of classroom environment assessments in school psychology: A British perspective. *Psychology in the Schools, 30*(3), 232–240.

Byrne, D. B., Hattie, J. A., & Fraser, B. J. (1986). Student perceptions of preferred classroom learning environment. *The Journal of Educational Research, 80*(1), 10–18.

Charalampous, K., & Kokkinos, C. M. (2017). The Greek Elementary "What Is Happening In this Class?" (G-EWIHIC): A three-phase multi-sample mixed methods study. *Studies in Educational Evaluation, 52*, 55–70.

Chionh, Y. H., & Fraser, B. J. (2009). Classroom environment, achievement, attitudes and self-esteem in geography and mathematics in Singapore. *International Research in Geographical and Environmental Education, 18*, 29–44.

Cleveland, B., & Fisher, K. (2013). The evaluation of physical learning environments: A critical review of the literature. *Learning Environments Research, 17*, 1–28.

Cleveland, B., & Fisher, K. (2014). The evaluation of physical learning environments: A critical review of the literature. *Learning Environments Research, 17*(1), 1–28.

Cohn, S. T., & Fraser, B. J. (2016). Effectiveness of student response systems in terms of learning environment, attitudes and achievement. *Learning Environments Research, 19*, 153–167.

Dorman, J. P. (2008). Use of multitrait-multimethod modelling to validate actual and preferred forms of the What Is Happening In this Class? (WIHIC) questionnaire. *Learning Environments Research, 11*, 179–197.

Dorman, J. P., & Fraser, B. J. (2009). Psychosocial environment and affective outcomes in technology-rich classrooms: Testing a causal model. *Social Psychology of Education, 12*, 77–99.

Fisher, D. L., & Fraser, B. J. (1981). Validity and use of my class inventory. *Science Education, 65*, 145–156.

Fisher, K. (Ed.). (2016). *The translational design of schools: An evidence-based approach to aligning pedagogy and learning environments* (Advances in Learning Environments Research Series). Rotterdam, The Netherlands: Sense Publishers.

Fisher, K. (in press). *The translational design of universities: An evidence-based approach* (Advances in Learning Environments Research Series). Leiden, The Netherlands: Brill Sense.

Fraser, B. J. (1981). Using environmental assessments to make better classrooms. *Journal of Curriculum Studies, 13*(2), 131–144.

Fraser, B. J. (1988). Learning environment instruments: Development, validity and applications. *Learning Environment Research, 1*(1), 35–57.

Fraser, B. J. (1990). *Individualised classroom environment questionnaire*. Melbourne: Australian Council for Educational Research.

Fraser, B. J. (2001). Twenty thousand hours. *Learning Environments Research, 4*(1), 1–5.

Fraser, B. J. (2012). Classroom learning environments: Retrospect, context and prospect. In B. J. Fraser, K. G. Tobin, & C. J. McRobbie (Eds.), *Second international handbook of science education* (pp. 1191–1232). New York, NY: Springer.

Fraser, B. J. (2014). Classroom learning environments: Historical and contemporary perspectives. In N. G. Lederman & S. K. Abell (Eds.), *Handbook of research on science education* (Vol. II, pp. 104–119). New York, NY: Routledge.

Fraser, B. J., & Aldridge, J. M. (2017). Improving classrooms through assessment of learning environments. In J . P. Bakken (Ed.), *Classrooms volume 1: Assessment practices for teachers and student improvement strategies* (pp. 91–107). New York, NY: Nova Science Publishers.

Fraser, B. J., Aldridge, J. M., & Adolphe, F. S. G. (2010). A cross-national study of secondary science classroom environments in Australia and Indonesia. *Research in Science Education, 40*, 551–571.

Fraser. B. J., & Butts, W. L. (1982). Relationship between perceived levels of classroom individualization and science-related attitudes. *Journal of Research in Science Teaching, 19*(2), 143–154.

Fraser, B. J., & Fisher, D. L. (1982). Predicting students' outcomes from their perceptions of classroom psychosocial environment. *American Educational Research Journal, 19*, 498–518.

Fraser, B. J., & Fisher, D. L. (1983). Development and validation of short forms of some instruments measuring student perceptions of actual and preferred classroom learning environment. *Science Education, 67*(1), 115–131.

Fraser, B. J., & Fisher, D. L. (1983). Student achievement as a function of person-environment fit: A regression surface analysis. *British Journal of Educational Psychology, 53*, 89–99.

Fraser, B. J., Giddings, G. J., & McRobbie, C. J. (1995). Evolution and validation of a personal form of an instrument for assessing science laboratory classroom environments. *Journal of Research in Science Teaching, 32*(4), 399–422.

Fraser, B. J., & Lee, S. S. U. (2009). Science laboratory classroom environments in Korean high schools. *Learning Environments Research, 12*, 67–84.

Fraser, B. J., & McRobbie, C. J. (1995). Science laboratory classroom environments at schools and universities: A cross-national study. *Educational Research and Evaluation, 1*, 289–317.

Fraser, B. J., & O'Brien, P. (1985). Student and teacher perceptions of the environment of elementary-school classrooms. *Elementary School Journal, 85*, 567–580.

Fraser, B. J., & Treagust, D. F. (1986). Validity and use of an instrument for assessing classroom psychosocial environment in higher education. *Higher Education, 15*, 37–57.

Fraser, B. J., Treagust, D. F., & Dennis, N. C. (1986). Development of an instrument for assessing classroom psychosocial environment at universities and colleges. *Studies in Higher Education, 11*, 43–54.

Fraser, B. J., Williamson, J. C., & Tobin, K. (1987). Use of classroom and school climate scales in evaluating alternative high schools. *Teaching and Teacher Education, 3*, 219–231.

Giallousi, M., Gialamas, V., Spyrellis, N., & Pavlatou, E. A. (2010). Development, validation, and use of a Greek-language questionnaire for assessing learning environments in grade 10 chemistry classes. *International Journal of Science and Mathematics Education, 8*, 761–782.

Goh, S. C., & Fraser, B. J. (1998). Teacher interpersonal behaviour, classroom environment and student outcomes in primary mathematics in Singapore. *Learning Environments Research, 1*, 199–229.

Goh, S. C., & Fraser, B. J. (2000). Teacher interpersonal behavior and elementary students' outcomes. *Journal of Research in Childhood Education, 14*(2), 216–231.

Goh, S. F., & Fraser, B. J. (2016). Learning environment in Singapore primary school classrooms: The ideal and the real. In K. Wallace (Ed.), *Learning environments: Emerging theories, applications and future directions* (pp. 125–141). New York, NY: Nova Science Publishers.

Hasan, A., & Fraser, B. J. (2015). Effectiveness of teaching strategies for engaging adults who experienced childhood difficulties in learning mathematics. *Learning Environments Research, 18*, 1–13.

Helding, K. A., & Fraser, B. J. (2013). Effectiveness of NBC (National Board Certified) teachers in terms of learning environment, attitudes and achievement among secondary school students. *Learning Environments Research, 16*, 1–21.

Imms, W., Cleveland, B., & Fisher, K. (Eds.). (2016). *Evaluating learning environments: Snapshots of emerging issues, methods and knowledge* (Advances in Learning Environments Research Series). Rotterdam, The Netherlands: Sense Publishers.

Kim, H. B., Fisher, D. L., & Fraser, B. J. (2000). Classroom environment and teacher interpersonal behaviour in secondary science classes in Korea. *Evaluation and Research in Education, 14*, 3–22.

Khine, M. S., Fraser, B. J., Afari, E., Oo, Z., & Kyaw, T. T. (2018). Students' environment in tertiary science classrooms in Myanmar. *Learning Environments Research, 21*(1), 135–152.

Koh, N. K., & Fraser, B. J. (2014). Learning environment associated with use of mixed mode delivery model among secondary business studies students in Singapore. *Learning Environments Research, 17*(2), 157–171.

Koul, R. B., & Fisher, D. L. (2005). Cultural background and students' perceptions of science classroom learning environment and teacher interpersonal behaviour in Jammu, India. *Learning Environments Research, 8*, 195–211.

Leary, T. (1957). *An interpersonal diagnosis of personality*. New York, NY: Ronald Press Company.

Lewin, K. (1936). *Principles of topological psychology*. New York, NY: McGraw-Hill.

Lightburn, M. E., & Fraser, B. J. (2007). Classroom environment and student outcomes among students using anthropometry activities in high school science. *Research in Science and Technological Education, 25*, 153–166.

Lim, C.-T. D., & Fraser, B. J. (in press). Learning environments research in English classrooms. *Learning Environments Research*.

Liu, L., & Fraser, B. J. (2013). Development and validation of an English classroom learning environment inventory and its application in China. In M. S. Khine (Ed.), *Application of structural equation modeling in educational research and practice* (pp. 75–89). Rotterdam, The Netherlands: Sense Publishers.

Logan, K. A., Crump, B. J., & Rennie, L. J. (2006). Measuring the computer classroom environment: Lessons learned from using a new instrument. *Learning Environments Research, 9*, 67–93.

Majeed, A., Fraser, B. J., & Aldridge, J. M. (2002). Learning environment and its associations with student satisfaction among mathematics students in Brunei Darussalam. *Learning Environments Research, 5*, 203–226.

Martin-Dunlop, C., & Fraser, B. J. (2008). Learning environment and attitudes associated with an innovative course designed for prospective elementary teachers. *International Journal of Science and Mathematics Education, 6*, 163–190.

Moos, R. H. (1974). *The social climate scales: An overview*. Palo Alto, CA: Consulting Psychologists Press.

Moos, R. H., & Trickett, E. J. (1974). *Classroom environment scale manual*. Palo Alto, CA: Consulting Psychologists Press.

Nix, R. K., Fraser, B. J., & Ledbetter, C. E. (2005). Evaluating an integrated science learning environment using the Constructivist Learning Environment Survey (CLES). *Learning Environments Research, 8*, 109–133.

Peiro, M. M., & Fraser, B. J. (2009). Assessment and investigation of science learning environments in the early childhood grades. In M. Ortiz & C. Rubio (Eds.), *Educational evaluation: 21st century issues and challenges* (pp. 349–365). New York, NY: Nova Science Publishers.

Prain, V. (2018). Using quantitative methods to evaluate students' post-occupancy perceptions of personalised learning in an innovative learning environment. In S. Alterator & C. Deed (Eds.), *School space and its occupation: Conceptualising and evaluating innovative learning environments*. Leiden, The Netherlands: Brill Sense.

Rentoul, A. J., & Fraser, B. J. (1979). Conceptualization of enquiry-based or open classroom learning environments. *Journal of Curriculum Studies, 11*, 233–245.

Rijken, P. E., Fraser, B. J., Aldridge, J. M. (2016, April). *Effectiveness of teacher action research in improving learning environments*. Paper presented at Annual Meeting of American Educational Research Association, Washington, DC.

Rogers, J., & Fraser, B. J. (2013, April). *Sex and frequency of practical work as determinants of middle-school science students' attitudes and aspirations*. Paper presented at Annual Meeting of American Educational Research Association, San Francisco, CA.

Scott Houston, L., Fraser, B. J., & Ledbetter, C. E. (2008). An evaluation of elementary school science kits in terms of classroom environment and student attitudes. *Journal of Elementary Science Education, 20*, 29–47.

Sink, C. A., & Spencer, L. R. (2005). My class inventory: Short form as an accountability tool for elementary school counsellors to measure classroom climate. *Professional School Counseling, 9*, 37–48.

Sirrakos, G., & Fraser, B. J. (2017). A cross-national mixed-method study of reality pedagogy. *Learning Environments Research, 20*(2), 153–174.

Skordi, P. (in press). Assessment of the psychosocial learning environment of university statistics classrooms. In K. Fisher (Ed.), *The translational design of universities: An evidence-based approach*. Leiden, The Netherlands: Brill Sense.

Spinner, H., & Fraser, B. J. (2005). Evaluation of an innovative mathematics program in terms of classroom environment, student attitudes, and conceptual development. *International Journal of Science and Mathematics Education, 3*, 267–293.

Strayer, J. F. (2012). How learning in an inverted classroom influences cooperation, innovation and task orientation. *Learning Environments Research, 15*, 171–193.

Taylor, P. C., Fraser, B. J., & Fisher, D. L. (1997). Monitoring constructivist classroom learning environments. *International Journal of Educational Research, 27*, 293–302.

Teh, G. P. L., & Fraser, B. J. (1995). Development and validation of an instrument for assessing the psychosocial environment of computer-assisted learning classrooms. *Journal of Educational Computing Research, 12*(2), 177–193.

Walberg, H. J. (1970). A model for research on instruction. *School Review, 80*, 185–200.

Walberg, H. J., & Anderson, G. J. (1968). Classroom climate and individual learning. *Journal of Educational Psychology, 59*, 414–419.

Welch, W. W., & Walberg, H. J. (1972). A national experiment in curriculum evaluation. *American Educational Research Journal, 9*, 373–383.

Wolf, S. J., & Fraser, B. J. (2008). Learning environment, attitudes and achievement among middle-school science students using inquiry-based laboratory activities. *Research in Science Education, 38*, 321–341.

Wong, A. L. F., & Fraser, B. J. (1996). Environment-attitude associations in the chemistry laboratory classroom. *Research in Science and Technological Education, 14*, 91–102.

Wubbels, Th., & Brekelmans, M. (2012). Teacher–students relationships in the classroom. In B. J. Fraser, K. G. Tobin, & C. J. McRobbie (Eds.), *Second international handbook of science education* (pp. 1241–1255). New York, NY: Springer.

Zaragoza, J. M., & Fraser, B. J. (2017). Field-study classrooms as positive and enjoyable learning environments. *Learning Environments Research, 20*(1), 1–20.

CHAPTER 2

My Journey in the Learning Environments Research Community

Research on Teacher–Student Interactions and Relationships

Theo Wubbels
Utrecht University, Utrecht, The Netherlands

Attending the annual meeting of the American Educational Research Association (AERA) nearly every year has been an inspiring event in my professional and personal life. During these visits, I focused on three topics: teaching and teacher education, classroom management and learning environments research. This chapter highlights some of my experiences with the Special Interest Group (SIG): The Study of Learning Environments, which later was renamed as SIG 120: Learning Environments. The SIG has been of utmost importance in developing the program of research of our research group at Utrecht University in the Netherlands and the dissemination of its results worldwide. I position these experiences in the context of the developments of the research on teacher–student relationships and interactions that started in the science education group at Utrecht University. As of 1990, this group was part of the teacher education department and later the Faculty of Social and Behavioral Sciences in the same university. Through the years, other Dutch universities also participated, specifically Eindhoven University of Technology and Leiden University. I structure my experiences and the developments of the research chronologically starting from the time before my involvement in the SIG and completing it with a summary of what a 2018 contribution to a SIG session might be.

1. Pre-Learning Environments Stage

When I first participated in the annual meeting of the AERA back in 1985 in Chicago, I had hardly any knowledge of the evolving learning environments research tradition which I first experienced there. I had just finished my PhD on discipline problems of beginning teachers and the support that schools could provide for these teachers, and I presented a paper on it in Chicago (Wubbels, Créton, & Hooymayers, 1985).

© KONINKLIJKE BRILL NV, LEIDEN, 2019 | DOI:10.1163/9789004387720_002

I wrote that PhD thesis in collaboration with Hans Créton, a colleague to whom I'm indebted a lot because of his sharing with me his insights into the broad field of education and specifically into relationships and interaction processes in classrooms. We completed our PhDs with a jointly-written manuscript (Créton & Wubbels, 1984) for which he was responsible for more qualitative chapters and I was responsible for more quantitative chapters. A jointly written thesis was and is possible in the Netherlands, but that possibility is seldom used. I think that this is a pity because, through collaboration, nearly every research becomes stronger. In our case, the manuscript was strengthened through our complementary skills and orientations: Hans Créton was more creative and diverging, whereas I was more analytic and converging, which appeared to be an ideal combination for producing valuable and interesting research results. The thesis included a first step towards a theory on teacher–student interaction processes in the classroom, the design and evaluation of a support program for beginning teachers, the development of the original Dutch version of the Questionnaire on Teacher Interaction (QTI), descriptive results from administrating this questionnaire in four schools in the Netherlands, and a 100-page case study of one beginning teacher with severe discipline problems. We documented and analysed her experiences for a one-year period, the interactions with students and the support that she received from a university-based supervisor. My first involvement in AERA sparked my interest in translating our work into English, when the audience of my paper presentation thanked me for bringing Timothy Leary back to the US and through a meeting with an American colleague, Fred Pigge, who showed interest in the QTI.

Several elements of the thesis later were published in international journals. The first draft of a theory on classroom interaction processes was published in a paper on the systems communicative approach to classroom communication (Wubbels, Créton, & Holvast, 1988). It translated general communicative principles to the classroom context and later we illustrated, in a short form of the case study, how such concepts could be used to help teachers to overcome problems in their classes (Créton, Wubbels, & Hooymayers, 1989). We developed the support program to be run by schools without support from outside. It included mutual observation of lessons by peers, individual supervision with classroom observations and pre- and post-lesson interviews by trained supervisors, and finally sessions with all beginning teachers in a school to support each other in their often quite emotional experiences and to further develop strategies for analysing classroom interactions. The development and evaluation of the program had been reported in an international journal (Wubbels, Créton, Hooymayers, & Holvast, 1982) and later more substantively by Wubbels, Créton, and Hooymayers (1987). The latter paper reported a study with an experimental and control group that included pretest and posttest measures such as student perceived teacher clarity and teacher experienced stress and anxiety. Small positive effects were reported for the support program.

In 1985 at the AERA annual meeting, I presented a paper on our thesis to the special interest group on teaching and teacher education, now division K of AERA. It introduced the Model for Interpersonal Teacher Behavior that was based on the Leary model (Leary, 1957) and is now usually referred to as the Interpersonal Circle for the Teacher, IPC-T (e.g., Mainhard, 2015). In the model, teacher–student interactions are conceptualised in terms of the two basic dimensions of *agency* (i.e. dominance, interpersonal influence) and *communion* (friendliness, warmth), which was called proximity in 1985), which are aggregated as a weighted combination of levels of both factors. The IPC reflects all possible combinations of agency and communion (Figure 2.1) and is usually divided in eight octants describing eight different behaviour types. The eight octants reflect prototypical labels of behaviour that correspond to a specific blend of agency and communion. Octants on the right side of the model represent behaviours characterised by relatively high levels of communion, and behaviours in the upper portion of the model represent relatively high agentic behaviour. Octants near one another are positively correlated (e.g. dissatisfied and confrontational) whereas behaviours on the opposite sides of the IPC are negatively correlated (e.g. dissatisfied and helpful). An important characteristic of the model is that agency and communion are (theoretically and empirically) orthogonal (Fabrigar, Visser, & Browne, 1997). In other words, knowing the level of agency that a teacher conveys in class does not tell us how this agency is enacted; it could be through confrontational behaviour or through helpful behaviour, which reflect a similar level of agency but opposite values of communion.

The 1985 paper further summarised the development of the QTI (at that time called the QUIT Questionnaire for Interactional Teacher Behaviour) and how we measured student and teacher views of the teacher–student relationship. The original Dutch version consists of 77 items that are answered on a five-point scale ranging from 'Never/Not at all' to 'Always/Very'. The QTI assesses each of the octants of the IPC for the teacher representing different combinations of agentic and communal teacher behaviours. The QTI includes items such as 'This teacher acts hesitantly' and 'This teacher is strict'. A student's perception of these eight octants can be used to map not only idiosyncratic perceptions but also, in classroom aggregated form, the classroom interpersonal climate and finally, if summarised over several classes, a teacher's general interpersonal disposition (den Brok, Brekelmans, & Wubbels, 2006; Lüdtke et al., 2009).

The results from administrating the QTI in the 1985 paper included a first typology of teacher–student interaction types, data on best and worst teachers, comparisons of teacher and student views on teacher behaviour, and data on the behaviour for teachers with different amounts of experience. Many of the descriptive results were replicated later with larger samples and published, for example, in the PhD thesis by Mieke Brekelmans (1989) and in subsequent articles (e.g., Wubbels, Brekelmans, & Hooymayers, 1993).

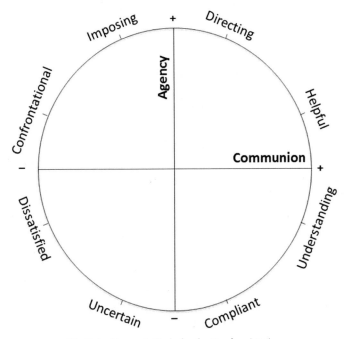

FIGURE 2.1   The Inter Personal Circle for the Teacher (IPC)

In our 1985 paper and several years thereafter, we used the term 'teacher behaviour' extensively and we were criticised for having a behavioural approach that disregards, for example, the importance of teacher thinking. We were seen as old-fashioned behaviourists who hadn't been aware of the negative connotations that the word behaviour had at that time and probably still has today for many people. We tried to cope with such criticisms in later years by, for example, by using 'interactions' instead of teacher and student behaviour, which had the additional advantage that it referred to the mutual influencing of these behaviours. The criticism certainly felt a bit unfair for us. Even in the 1985 paper, we already presented teachers' perceptions of their own behaviour and what they considered ideal, thus including what later was called teacher thinking into our analyses. However, the mere use of the word behaviour apparently put us in a tradition that we didn't feel we were in. This criticism is also an example of language problems that non-native speakers might have when starting to participate in the international research community; the Dutch translation of behaviour has a far more neutral connotation. In our contribution to the fourth conference of the International Study Association on Teacher Thinking (ISATT) in Nottingham in 1988 (Brekelmans, Wubbels, & Hooymayers, 1988), we introduced the expression teacher action (instead of behaviour) and referred to teacher thinking (instead of perceptions). Thus we firmly separated from behaviourist connotations.

2 Early Learning Environments SIG Stage

When in Chicago in 1985, I missed the first full program of AERA's Learning Environments SIG. During my first AERA annual meeting, I felt like a stranger in a new world, running all day from session to session because I had no idea what the best place for my research would be. In the 1985 AERA paper, I reported on the views of students (and teachers) of teacher behaviour and this was in the context of problems of beginning teachers. The natural home for presenting the paper for me therefore seemed to be the SIG on teaching and teacher education. I only learned about the learning environments SIG when, in 1986, my colleague and later PhD student, Ronnie Wierstra, visited several sessions of the learning environments SIG during the annual meeting of AERA in San Francisco. Ronnie had been working on classroom environment measures following the tradition of Barry Fraser's (2012) work and we co-authored a paper for the SIG on these measures (Wierstra, Jörg, & Wubbels, 1987). The instruments had been developed in the context of the evaluation of an innovative Dutch curriculum for physics education in the 1980s (PLON, Lijnse et al., 1990). Because of the features of that program, the three scales used were reality, participation and activity learning. Through Ronnie's experience, I was introduced to the developing learning environment scholars' community. I realised that part of my research could and should be framed as learning environments research. Through the first contacts with the learning environments SIG, I realised that one of the contributions of our work was the development of a learning environment instrument to measure students' and teachers' perceptions of the teacher–student relationship, an essential aspect of the learning environment or classroom social climate. So I was encouraged to submit a paper proposal for the 1987 SIG meeting (Wubbels, Brekelmans, &

Hermans, 1987), travelled to Washington and felt immediately well at home in the SIG community.

2.1 IPC and QTI Development

The first development of the model and of the questionnaire meant to represent this model was thoroughly described only in Dutch in our 1984 thesis. The first adaptation to another language started in 1985 when Fred Pigge was kind enough to administer the first English language pilot version of the QTI in US classrooms, which was a time-consuming process in an era without internet and email. The adaptation of the questionnaire for the English-speaking world really got off the ground with my first encounter with Jack Levy from George Mason University at the learning environments SIG at the AERA annual meeting in 1987. We started to work on it for many pilot rounds in Fairfax schools in the US, completed it in 1988, and finally published this 64-item version in 1991.

Participating in the SIG community helped me to build a network with researchers from other countries because of the strong international character of the SIG. In my 2015 presentation for the SIG's business meeting, I showed that the third volume of the SIG's paper collection *The study of learning environments* (Fraser, 1987) included six nationalities and that Fisher and Khine's (2006) book *Contemporary approaches to research on learning environments: World views* encompassed 15 countries. This international character gave me, and later my younger colleagues, the opportunity to work for some time with colleagues at Curtin University in Perth, Australia. Such an experience was not only essential for non-native English speakers to develop the language skills needed to participate in an international research community, but also to learn from other learning environment researchers. Specifically during one of my visits in 1993, I worked on developing the 48-item version of the QTI (Wubbels, 1993) through which the dissemination of the QTI as a research instrument got a strong boost. After that visit and the publication of the shorter questionnaire the QTI was disseminated from the Netherlands, Australia and the US into many countries (see Wubbels et al., 2012) such as Brunei, Canada, China (Sun, Mainhard, & Wubbels, 2017), Cyprus, India, Indonesia, Israel, Italy (Passini, Molinari, & Speltini, 2015), Poland, Singapore, Turkey, Thailand and UK.[1]

As an aside, the 1993 visit to Perth gave me also the opportunity to collect videotapes of teacher–student interactions in English-speaking classes. Such recordings were of utmost importance for the workshops that we started to give internationally on the use of the model for interpersonal teacher behaviour in, for example, supervision of (student) teachers.

2.2   Adaptation Problems

The Dutch and US/Australian versions of the QTI were developed after several pilot administrations and analyses (Wubbels & Levy, 1991). Extensive interviews with students and teachers were conducted and items were repeatedly revised in pursuit of satisfactory psychometric properties. The goal was to produce an instrument with high alpha reliabilities for each scale, as well as a pattern of scale correlations that represented the circumplex nature of the model. Employing a similar comprehensive process, Telli, den Brok, and Cakiroglu (2007) developed a Turkish version of the QTI and Wei, den Brok, and Zhou (2009) developed a Chinese one. The design procedure for these two versions were noteworthy in that the authors did not simply translate the items from one language to another, but rather adapted them to the cultural environment as well. Sun, Mainhard, and Wubbels (2017) showed, that despite these efforts, even this Chinese version needed improvements. Most QTI adaptations, however, were not as thorough and usually involved only translation and occasional back translation. It is understandable that scholars adapting the QTI to other languages were insufficiently aware of the extensive interviewing involved in the development of the QTI and the efforts to design the items in such a way that they were representations of the two-dimensional model, because unfortunately we did not report the development of the questionnaire in an international journal. This has led to problems in adaptations of the QTI to other languages (Wubbels et al., 2012).

In addition to the limited attention to the circumplex framework of the model when just translating the QTI, two characteristics of the Dutch QTI and later the US version hindered adequate development of adaptations in other languages. Wubbels and Levy (1991) provided an indication of these challenges in their comparison of the Dutch and US versions. First, the correlations between scales deviated from that expected of an ideal circumplex: the correlation between the Directing and Imposing scales was too low, whereas the correlation between Helpful and Understanding was too high. Therefore the distribution of the scales in the circle was uneven (Wubbels & Levy, 1991). Unless the translators were aware of these weaknesses, adaptations of the QTI to other languages risked exacerbating them. Next, for the Compliant scale, some items had deliberately been chosen because they tended to correlate highly with Understanding and others with Uncertain. Taken together, this resulted in adequate correlations with the two adjacent scales, but a translation might distort the importance of one item over another, thus further distorting the relationship between scales. Finally, misunderstandings caused by the sector titles (Wubbels et al., 2012) might have further hindered the development of sound versions in other languages. As a result of these difficulties, the psychometric qualities of translated versions are usually lower than those of the Dutch, US/Australian and Turkish versions (see e.g., Kokkinos, Charalambous, & Davazoglou, 2009; Passini, Molinari, & Speltini, 2015).

3 Further Involvement in the SIG

From 1987 onwards, I became a regular participant in the AERA Learning Environments SIG and, through entering this community, I was encouraged to connect student perceptions of interpersonal relationships and the world of learning environments. Thus I started to understand how my research fitted into a broader picture. In my perception of the learning environments SIG, the original focus was heavily on student questionnaires. Quite soon, however, the use of other more-qualitative measures and the perceptions of others involved in the classroom, especially the teacher, were emphasised (e.g., Matyas, Tobin, & Fraser, 1989). In our own work reported in the 1985 paper, observations already were included and the QTI was used to measure not only students' but also teachers' perceptions of the relationship with students. Student perceptions of the preferred environment were part and parcel of learning environments research from the beginning (e.g., Fraser, 1989). Not being knowledgeable about that learning environments tradition, we presented in the 1985 paper data on what we called teacher ideals for the teacher behaviour. After learning about other learning environments research, we then started to understand that, in line with that tradition, we could have renamed these teacher ideals as teacher perceptions of the preferred teacher. For student perceptions, we presented data on their best teacher. We deliberately didn't ask students what their preferred environment was because we wanted to collect data referring to what realistically is possible for teachers to achieve in the classroom. Therefore we asked students to think about their best teacher and complete the questionnaire for that teacher. Thus our measure for student preferences differed from what was commonly used in learning environments studies.

The SIG's sessions gave me the opportunity to learn about developments in the field of learning environments studies and later, through being the European Editor for the SIG's journal *Learning Environments Research*, I had the (admittedly time-consuming) opportunity to stay at the front of developments. Such editorships require reading many different and diverse contributions, stimulating my thinking about the field and sharpening ideas. SIG sessions not only helped me to learn about the field, but also offered the opportunity to present our own developments, such as employing mixed methods research (including observations, interviews and student questionnaires) and advances in the mostly quantitative methods applied in the Utrecht research group that were specifically developed and encouraged by Mieke Brekelmans. These included, for example, using LISREL for testing circumplex models (Wubbels & Levy, 1991) and multilevel analyses. Such multilevel analyses were already included in the thesis by Mieke Brekelmans published before multilevel software was readily available (Brekelmans, 1989; Levy, Wubbels, den Brok, & Brekelmans, 2003). These methods have now been developed in advanced data analyses through multilevel structural equation modelling (e.g., Breeman et al., 2015), employing the CircE program for testing circular models (e.g., CircE; Grassi, Luccio, & Di Blas, 2010; Pennings et al., 2014a) and advanced scoring of interactions on the two dimensions on a second-to-second basis with the help of the joystick method (Pennings et al., 2014b, see next section).

Participation in the learning environments SIG has strongly guided and supported my research activity and accomplishments. Alongside the pressures in Dutch universities to make educational research more visible internationally, the SIG not only sparked my interest in international publications, but also helped to realise such publications. When I started to work in educational research back in 1980 in the Netherlands, the overwhelming majority of the research results were published in Dutch. In that decade, the pressure on researchers specifically in education to publish internationally gradually was built up and, by the end of that decade and through my learning environments contacts, among others, I had been able to change not only my own publication habits but also those of my colleagues. Publishing in English became the standard in the 1990s, even to such a degree that I had to remind my research group that we also had a responsibility towards Dutch teachers, teacher educators and policy makers.

The SIG furthermore has been very important for encouraging publication of learning environments research results by offering the opportunity to publish papers presented at AERA first in the yearly collection of papers in the books *The study of learning environments* and later in the journal *Learning Environments Research*. Such publication possibilities have advanced the field and the careers of many learning environments researchers. The possibility to send in papers for the SIG's annual Best Paper Award was another encouragement for completing the conference papers and strengthening their quality.

4   Current Contributions to Learning Environments Research

4.1   *Interpersonal Theory*
Nowadays we firmly place our model of teacher–student relationships and interactions in the tradition of interpersonal theory (Horowitz & Strack,

2010) as a fine-grained scrutiny of teacher behaviour and students' general perceptions of that behaviour. We consider our model to be a particular instance or application of the interpersonal theory in the field of education. Whereas interpersonal theory primarily was used in dyadic relationships such as romantic or parent–child interactions, we used it for a description of one (teacher) to a group (class). Analogous to the interpersonal circle for the teacher, also such a circle describing student behaviours has been developed (Pennings, submitted; see Figure 2.2). The models for the perceptions of teacher and students behaviour usually are used to map both interactions (Pennings et al., 2014b) and interpersonal perceptions of a teacher's general behaviour in class (e.g., Mainhard, 2015; Wubbels et al., 2014). Different from our 1985 paper, we now clearly distinguish between interactions or behaviour and relationships or general perceptions of behaviour and refer to these often as micro-level variables (interactions or behaviours) and macro level variables (relationships). According to dynamic systems theory, interactions are not only the building blocks of relationships (Granic & Patterson, 2006), but relationships, in turn, also constrain interactions (Hollenstein & Lewis, 2006).

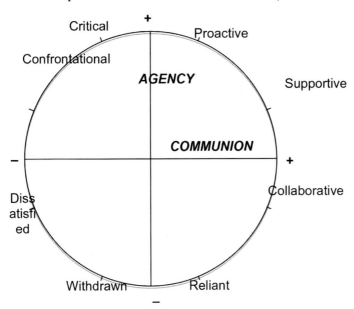

FIGURE 2.2   Interpersonal circle for students

Our involvement in the community of interpersonal psychology researchers introduced us to an advanced measurement tool for interactions: Continuous Assessment of Interpersonal Dynamics (CAID; Lizdek, Woody, Sadler, & Rehman, 2016; Sadler et al., 2009). This approach captures interpersonal dynamics as a continuous, contextualised flow of behaviour based on continuous coding of videotaped behaviours using a computer joystick apparatus. Behaviour is coded as a specific blend of Agency and Communion (Markey, Lowmeister, & Eichler, 2010). Figure 2.3 provides an example of the results of such measurements (from Pennings et al., submitted).

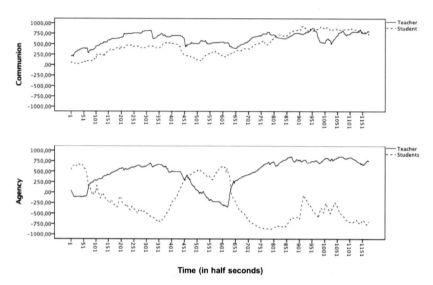

FIGURE 2.3   Example of time series measurement every 0.5 seconds of teacher and students for communion and agency (dotted line represents students and continuous line represents the teacher)

4.2   Development of Relationships: Knowledge until 2015

We organised the first International Conference on Interpersonal Relationships in Education (ICIRE) in 2010 in Boulder, Colorado in the US in conjunction with the AERA annual meeting. This conference was heavily influenced by the participation of members of the AERA Learning Environments SIG. In the last chapter of the book that was published after this conference (Wubbels et al., 2012), we listed challenges for future research on interpersonal relationships in classroom learning environments. I now would summarise one of these as follows. From previous research, we know that teacher–student relationships that are characterised by a combination of high levels of teacher agency and communion are conducive to learning. Students who attend classes with relatively high average levels of teacher agency and communion show greater cognitive achievement and more positive subject-related attitudes than those whose teachers are rated lower on these dimensions (e.g., Wubbels et al., 2016). A challenge for future research is to determine how teachers can create such positive relationships. As teacher–student relationships can be understood as the generalised interpersonal meaning that students and teachers attach to their interactions with each other, it is important to study how these generalised perceptions and the interactions are related and more specifically how these interactions work as building blocks for relationships.

For coping with this challenge, research mapping interactions in terms of both teacher and student positions in the IPC is needed. A first step in this was set by Mainhard et al. (2012), following earlier work by van Tartwijk, Brekelmans, Wubbels, Fisher, and Fraser (1989). They developed scoring instruments for both teacher and class on the agency and communion dimension and used these to score teacher and student positions in the IPC. When both teacher and class position in the IPC are measured, interpersonal complementarity can be used to describe the adaptation or alignment between the teacher and class behaviour. Interpersonal complementarity in terms of agency is defined as reciprocity and tends towards oppositeness. For example, if a teacher takes control (high agency), students usually tend to listen and go along with the teacher (low agency). Interpersonal complementarity in terms of communion is defined through correspondence and tends towards sameness (Sadler et al., 2009). For example, if the teacher acts friendly towards the students (high communion), it is likely that the students act friendly towards the teacher too (high communion), and also student hostility might invite teacher hostility and vice versa.

In our chapter in the second edition of the *Handbook on Classroom Management* (Wubbels et al., 2014), we summarised what is known about the development of relationships through interactions based on three studies. We now add to this two studies by Pennings et al. (2014a, 2014b). First, Vick Whittaker and Jones Harden (2010) reported only weak associations between teacher–student relationships and observed interactions. The strongest (negative) association was found between conflict in the relationship and positive interactions.

Mainhard et al. (2011) showed that supportive teacher behaviours in one lesson were positively correlated to the teacher–student relationship in terms of communion during that same lesson and also in the lesson a week later. These supportive behaviours, however, were not correlated with the relationship in terms of teacher agency. Notably, coercive teacher behaviours in one lesson were negatively correlated with the relationship in terms of communion during that lesson and the lesson a week later, but tended not to correlate with the level of a teacher's agency in the classroom. Thus, when a teacher showed coercive behaviour in order to improve the teacher–student relationship, this had a counterproductive effect. Mainhard et al. (2012) compared interactions in one classroom with a positive and one classroom with a negative teacher–student relationship. Most of the time, interaction in both classrooms was characterised by teacher behaviours on agency being somewhat higher than student behaviours, and by complementary teacher and student communion behaviours that were medium to high. This might reflect the commonly-assumed social hierarchy in classrooms, which combines legitimate teacher power with a basically non-oppositional attitude among both teacher and students. One difference between the interactions in the two classrooms was that, in more positive teacher–student relationship interactions high teacher communion behaviour was frequently observed, whereas reciprocated hostile interaction behaviours only occurred within the less-positive teacher–student relationship. Mainhard et al. (2012) also suggested that variability in interaction might explain differences between positive and negative teacher–student relationships. Interactions varied far more within the less favourable than in the more favourable relationship.

Similar to the Mainhard et al. (2012) study, Pennings et al. (2014b) compared teacher–student interactions in the classes of two teachers with very different teacher–student relationships. In the first, the teacher was seen by the students as repressive (high on agency and low on communion) and, in the other, as tolerant (high on communion and low on agency). Three fragments of a lesson were analysed: the lesson start, a situation when the teacher was dissatisfied with the student behaviour (e.g., the student did not listen to the teacher), and a situation when the teacher seemed to feel satisfied (e.g., laughing or joking). Micro-level behaviours of both teachers and students were similar to how their behaviour was characterised at the macro-level (i.e. repressive vs. tolerant). In the classes of both these teachers, students' behaviours were rather stable and comparable in their variation in agency but, in the repressive teacher's class, students fluctuated more in their level of communion shown towards the teacher. So, in a repressive teacher's class, students might act friendly and unfriendly during a 10-minute lesson fragment whereas, in the tolerant teacher's lesson, that variation was smaller and more to the communion side of the circle. The interactions between teacher and class behaviour largely showed patterns following the complementarity principle (as displayed in Figure 2.3), with three exceptions. In the tolerant teacher's interactions in the negative situation, there was similar behaviour on the agency dimension (teacher and students competing in the negatively perceived situations for power in class). In the repressive teacher's interactions, there was no complementarity in the lesson start and, in the positive situation, the opposite occurred (the teacher being unfriendly and the student friendly). Finally, interactions of the tolerant teacher were less predictable than those of the repressive teacher in the positive situation, but more predictable in the lesson start and the negative situation.

Finally, Pennings et al. (2014a) found that micro-level interpersonal teacher behaviour was related to the macro-level teacher–student relationships. The average micro-level level of agency and communion in teacher behaviour and the macro-level agency and communion characterising the teachers–student relationship were very highly correlated. Furthermore, for teachers with more desirable teacher–student relationships (i.e. high on agency and communion), interactions tended to be located in the same or adjacent area (octant) that characterised the quality of their teacher–student relationship. For teachers with less desirable teacher–student relationships, however, there was no stable tendency for the interaction. Pennings et al. (2014a) found that, for the latter teachers, the interactions were much more variable in terms of the number of behaviour changes than for teachers with desirable relationships and these interactions were also less predictable. Regarding the relationship between micro-level and macro-level, variability and predictability in micro-level interpersonal teacher behaviour was only related to the level of communion that characterises the teacher–student relationship. The less variability and the more predictability, the higher was the level of communion in the relationships. This result implies that variability is not a desirable characteristic of teachers' behaviour towards students, whereas it is a characteristic of behaviours in healthy dyadic relationships.

4.3 *Development of Relationships: Knowledge after 2015*

What could a presentation in the AERA Learning Environments SIG look like in 2018? Since 2015, another study by Heleen Pennings and her colleagues have moved this field further. Pennings et al. (2018) observed interpersonal teacher and student behaviour, using Continuous Assessment of Interpersonal Dynamics. This study with a sample of 35 teachers confirmed that generally, in the interactions in the first 10 minutes of a lesson, there was complementarity (sameness regarding communion, oppositeness regarding agency). Patterns of teacher and students' behaviour, on average, were synchronised with each other. It is important to know if teachers or students are in the lead when there is complementarity. Do teachers high on agency make students be low on agency or invite students low on agency to be high on agency? Similarly, for the communion dimension, the question is: Do teachers become angry because of students' misbehaviour or is it the other way around? Do students behave friendly because of teacher friendliness or is it the other way around? The answer to this question of 'Who is leading whom?' can be seen from the interaction plots in Figure 2.3 and quantitative measures such as phase (Pennings et al., 2018). It appeared that classrooms had a varied pattern regarding who was leading the interactions during the lesson start. In 20% of the classrooms, the teacher led on both communion and agency and, in 26% of the classrooms, the teacher followed students on both agency and communion. In 20% of the classrooms, the teacher was leading on agency and following the students on communion, and in 34% the teacher was following students on agency and is leading on communion. Importantly, in classrooms with a more preferred teacher–student relationships, teachers with a leading pattern on agency were more prominent. Also, teachers in such classrooms were better able to refrain from hostility and subordinate behaviour (when facing hostile and dominant student behaviour). That means that they were able to break unfavourable patterns of complementarity. A next step in this line of research will be to gather data with multiple measurements of both interactions and the teacher–student relationship. When such data are available, we will again come closer to answers to the question about in what way interactions are the building blocks for relationships; that is, how relationships develop from interactions.

5   Concluding Remarks

In concluding this chapter, I want to mention briefly three other communities that influenced our work, one of which also prominently featured during my visits to AERA annual meetings. First and most noticeable, our work originated from the study of problems of beginning teachers which were of concern at the beginning of our research program as well as nowadays in classroom management (Jensen et al., 2012; Veenman, 1984). Teacher–student interactions and relationships are crucial for good classroom management and for creating a healthy classroom atmosphere. Because research on these relationships can be seen as one of six approaches to studying classroom management (Wubbels, 2015), the AERA SIG Classroom Management was also a natural and important outlet and inspiration for me. At several annual meetings of AERA, I had a hard time choosing between sessions and business meetings of the SIG's Learning Environments and Classroom Management.

Second, the Learning Environments SIG introduced me to the international world of science education researchers. Originally many participants in the Learning Environments SIG had a background in science education research and I originally also came from science (i.e. physics) education. Thus my work on teacher–student relationships became known among other science education researchers and opened up a world of contacts in many countries that helped in disseminating my research to the science education community.

For example, our work was included in the International Handbooks of Science Education (Wubbels & Brekelmans, 1998, 2012) and I was interviewed by Peter Fensham on the impact of my work in science education (Fensham, 2004). When I attended my second annual meeting of AERA in 1987 in Washington, I combined this with my first visit to the annual meeting of the National Association for Research in Science Teaching (NARST). Given my original training in physics and my consequent work as a physics teacher and researcher in physics education, this was an excellent combination.

Finally, our work is also related to the world of developmental and educational psychology in its focus on student motivation, emotional learning and achievement. Our group studied how aspects of social relationships contribute to children's social and academic functioning, with a focus on the teacher and recently also on peers (Hendrickx et al., 2016). We reported the teacher influence in a chapter in Wentzel and Ramani's (2016) *Handbook of Social Influences in School Contexts* (Wubbels et al., 2016). It is striking that the traditions of the Learning Environments SIG and those of developmental and educational psychology have so seldom been either connected or integrated. Both traditions in fact could learn from and strengthen each other.

This chapter has shown some of the theoretical and empirical developments among the research group studying teacher–student interactions and relationships at Utrecht University in the Netherlands. These interactions and relationships are elements of the classroom learning environment and the developments have been placed into the context of the Learning Environments SIG of AERA. I showed how these developments have been nurtured by my participation in the first 30 years of this SIG's community and, as an aside, by the interpersonal psychology tradition, the Classroom Management SIG, and the worlds of science education research and developmental and educational psychology. The learning environments SIG contributed for 30 years to our research and my career and I trust that the next 30 years will be as successful for the next generation of researchers on teacher–student interactions and relationships.

Note

1   The QTI was intended originally for use in secondary education and formed the basis of several new versions such as for primary education (e.g., Goh & Fraser, 1996), early primary education (Zijlstra, Wubbels, Brekelmans, & Koomen, 2013) and higher education teachers (e.g., Soerjaningsih, Fraser, & Aldridge, 2002), supervisors of student teachers (Kremer-Hayon & Wubbels, 1993a) and school

managers (Questionnaire on Principal Interaction, Kremer-Hayon & Wubbels, 1993b; Fisher & Cresswell, 1998). The instrument also formed the starting point for adaptations that are being used in post-compulsory education (Hockley & Harkin, 2000) and in supervision of doctoral students (Mainhard, Van der Rijst, Van Tartwijk, & Wubbels, 2009).

References

Breeman, L. D., Wubbels, Th., van Lier, P. A. C., Verhulst, F. C., van der Ende, J., Maras, A., Hopman, J. A. B., & Tick, N. T. (2015). Teacher characteristics, social classroom relationships, and children's social, emotional, and behavioral classroom adjustment in special education. *Journal of School Psychology, 53*(1), 87–103.

Brekelmans, M. (1989). *Interpersonal teacher behaviour in the classroom*. Utrecht: WCC.

Brekelmans, M., Wubbels, Th., & Hooymayers, H. P. (1988). *Teacher cognitions and interpersonal teacher behaviour* (pp. 19–23). Proceedings of the fourth ISATT Conference, Nottingham.

Créton, H. A., & Wubbels, Th. (1984). *Discipline problems with beginning teachers* [in Dutch]. Utrecht: WCC.

Créton, H. A., Wubbels, Th., & Hooymayers, H. P. (1989). Escalated disorderly situations in the classroom and the improvement of these situations. *Teaching and Teacher Education, 5*(3), 205–216.

den Brok, P., Brekelmans, M., & Wubbels, Th. (2006). Multilevel issues in studies using students' perceptions of learning environments: The case of the questionnaire on teacher interaction. *Learning Environments Research, 9*(3), 199–213.

Fabrigar, L. R., Visser, P. S., & Browne, M. W. (1997). Conceptual and methodological issues in testing the circumplex structure of data in personality and social psychology. *Personality and Social Psychology Review, 1*, 184–203.

Fensham, P. J. (2004). *Defining an identity*. Dordrecht: Springer.

Fisher, D., & Cresswell, J. (1998). Actual and ideal principal interpersonal behaviour. *Learning Environments Research, 1*, 231–247.

Fisher, D. L., & Khine, M. S. (Eds.). (2006). *Contemporary approaches to research on learning environments: Worldviews*. Singapore: World Scientific Publishing.

Fraser, B. J. (Ed.). (1987). *The study of learning environments* (Vol. 3). Perth: West Australian Institute of Technology.

Fraser, B. J. (1989). Twenty years of classroom climate work: Progress and prospect. *Journal of Curriculum Studies, 21*(4), 307–327.

Fraser, B. J. (2012). Classroom learning environments: Retrospect, context and prospect. In B. J. Fraser, K. G. Tobin, & C. J. McRobbie (Eds.), *Second international handbook of science education* (pp. 1191–1232). New York, NY: Springer.

Goh, S. C., & Fraser, B. J. (1996). Validation of an elementary school version of the questionnaire on teacher interaction. *Psychological Reports, 79*, 515–522.

Granic, I., & Patterson, G. R. (2006). Towards a comprehensive model of antisocial development: A dynamic systems approach. *Psychological Review, 113*(1), 101–131.

Grassi, M., Luccio, R., & Di Blas, L. (2010). CircE: An R implementation of Browne's circular stochastic process model. *Behavior Research Methods, 42*(1), 55–73.

Hendrickx, M. M., Mainhard, M. T., Boor-Klip, H. J., Cillessen, A. H., & Brekelmans, M. (2016). Social dynamics in the classroom: Teacher support and conflict and the peer ecology. *Teaching and Teacher Education, 53*, 30–40.

Hockley, M., & Harkin, J. (2000). Communicating with students with learning difficulties in further education. *Educational Action Research, 8*(2), 341–360.

Hollenstein, T., & Lewis, M. D. (2006). A state space analysis of emotion and flexibility in parent–child interactions. *Emotion, 6*(4), 663–669.

Horowitz, M. L., & Strack, S. (Eds.). (2010). *Handbook of interpersonal psychology*. New York, NY: Wiley.

Jensen, B., Sandoval-Hernández, A., Knoll, S., & Gonzalez, E. J. (2012). *The experience of new teachers: Results from TALIS 2008*. Paris: OECD Publishing.

Kokkinos, C. M., Charalambous, K., & Davazoglou, A. (2009). Interpersonal teacher behaviour in primary school classrooms: A cross-cultural validation of a Greek translation of the questionnaire on teacher interaction. *Learning Environments Research, 12*, 101–114.

Kremer-Hayon, L., & Wubbels, Th. (1993a). Supervisors' interpersonal behavior and student teachers' satisfaction. In Th. Wubbels & J. Levy (Eds.), *Do you know what you look like?* (pp. 123–135). London: Falmer Press.

Kremer-Hayon, L., & Wubbels, Th. (1993b). Principals' interpersonal behavior and teachers' satisfaction. In Th. Wubbels & J. Levy (Eds.), *Do you know what you look like?* (pp. 113–122). London: Falmer Press.

Leary, T. (1957). *An interpersonal diagnosis of personality*. New York, NY: Ronald Press Company.

Levy, J., Wubbels, Th., den Brok, P., & Brekelmans, M. (2003). Students' perceptions of interpersonal aspects of the learning environment. *Learning Environments Research, 6*(1), 5–36.

Lijnse, P. L., Kortland, K., Eijkelhof, H., Genderen, D. V., & Hooymayers, H. P. (1990). A thematic physics curriculum: A balance between contradictory curriculum forces. *Science Education, 74*(1), 95–103.

Lizdek, I., Sadler, P., Woody, E., Ethier, N., & Malet, G. (2012). Capturing the stream of behavior: A computer joystick method for coding interpersonal behavior continuously over time. *Social Science Computer Review, 30*(4), 513–521.

Lüdtke, O., Robitzsch, A., Trautwein, U., & Kunter, M. (2009). Assessing the impact of learning environments: How to use student ratings of classroom or school characteristics in multilevel modeling. *Contemporary Educational Psychology, 34,* 120–131.

Mainhard, M. T., Brekelmans, M., den Brok, P., & Wubbels, Th. (2011). The development of the classroom social climate during the first months of the school year. *Contemporary Educational Psychology, 36,* 190–200.

Mainhard, M. T., Pennings, H. J. M., Wubbels, Th., & Brekelmans, M. (2012). Mapping control and affiliation in teacher-student interaction with state space grids. *Teaching and Teacher Education, 28,* 1027–1037.

Mainhard, T. (2015). Liking a tough teacher: Interpersonal characteristics of teaching and students' achievement goals. *School Psychology International, 36*(6), 559–574.

Mainhard, T., van der Rijst, R., van Tartwijk, J., & Wubbels, Th. (2009). A model for the supervisor doctoral student relationship. *Higher Education, 58*(7), 359–373.

Markey, P. M., Lowmaster, S. E., & Eichler, W. C. (2010). A real-time assessment of interpersonal complementarity. *Personal Relationships, 17,* 13–25.

Matyas, M. L., Tobin, K., & Fraser, B. J. (Eds.). (1989). *Looking into windows: Qualitative research in science education.* Washington, DC: American Association for the Advancement of Science.

Passini, S., Molinari, L., & Speltini, G. (2015). A validation of the questionnaire on teacher interaction in Italian secondary school students: The effect of positive relations on motivation and academic achievement. *Social Psychology of Education, 18*(3), 547–559.

Pennings, H. J. M., Brekelmans, M., Sadler, P., Claessens, L. C. A., van der Want, A. C., & van Tartwijk, J. (2018). Interpersonal adaptation in teacher-student interaction. *Learning and Instruction, 55,* 41–57.

Pennings, H. J. M., Brekelmans, M., Wubbels, Th., van der Want, A. C., Claessens, L. C., & van Tartwijk, J. (2014a). A nonlinear dynamical systems approach to real-time teacher behavior: Differences between teachers. *Nonlinear Dynamics, Psychology, and Life Sciences, 18*(1), 23–45.

Pennings, H. J. M., van Tartwijk, J., Wubbels, Th., Claessens, L. C., van der Want, A. C., & Brekelmans, M. (2014b). Real-time teacher–student interactions: A dynamic systems approach. *Teaching and Teacher Education, 37,* 183–193.

Sadler, P., Ethier, N., Gunn, G. R., Duong, D., & Woody, E. (2009). Are we on the same wavelength? Interpersonal complementarity as shared cyclical patterns during interactions. *Journal of Personality and Social Psychology, 97*(6), 1005–1020.

Soerjaningsih, W., Fraser, B. J., & Aldridge, J. M. (2002, April). *Instructor-student interpersonal behavior and student outcomes at the university level in Indonesia.* Paper presented at the Annual Meeting of the American Educational Research Association, New Orleans, LA.

Sun, X., Mainhard, T., & Wubbels, Th. (2017). Development and evaluation of a Chinese version of the Questionnaire on Teacher Interaction (QTI). *Learning Environments Research, 21*(1), 1–17.

Telli, S., den Brok, P., & Cakiroglu, J. (2007). Students' perceptions of science teachers' interpersonal behaviour in secondary schools: Development of a Turkish version of the questionnaire on teacher interaction. *Learning Environments Research, 10,* 115–129.

van Tartwijk, J., Brekelmans, M., Wubbels, Th., Fisher, D. L., & Fraser, B. J. (1998). Students' perceptions of teacher interpersonal style: The front of the classroom as the teacher's stage. *Teaching and Teacher Education, 14*(6), 607–617.

Veenman, S. (1984). Perceived problems of beginning teachers. *Review of Educational Research, 54*(2), 143–178.

Vick Whittaker, J. E., & Jones Harden, B. (2010). Beyond ABCs and 123 s: Enhancing teacher–child relationship quality to promote children's behavioral development. NHSA *Dialog, 13,* 185–191.

Wei, M., den Brok, P., & Zhou, Y. (2009). An investigation of teacher interpersonal behaviour and student achievement in English as a Foreign Language (EFL) classrooms in China. *Learning Environments Research, 12*(3), 157–174.

Wentzel, K. R., & Ramani, G. B. (Eds.). (2016). *Handbook of social influences in school contexts: Social-emotional, motivation, and cognitive outcomes.* New York, NY: Routledge.

Wierstra, R. F. A., Jörg, A. G. D., & Wubbels, Th. (1987). Contextual and individually perceived learning environment in curriculum evaluation. In B. J. Fraser (Ed.), *The study of learning environments 2* (pp. 31–41). Perth: Curtin University of Technology.

Wubbels, Th. (1993). *Teacher–student relationships in science and mathematics classes.* Perth: Curtin University of Technology, National Key Centre for School Science and Mathematics.

Wubbels, Th. (2015). A cross-cultural perspective on classroom management. In M. Hayden, J. Levy, & J. Thompson (Eds.), *The Sage handbook of research in international education* (2nd ed., pp. 261–274). Los Angeles, CA: Sage Publications.

Wubbels, Th., Brekelmans, J. M. G., & Hermans, J. J. (1987). Teacher behavior, an important aspect of the learning environment? In B. J. Fraser (Ed.), *The study of learning environments* (Vol. 3, pp. 10–25). Perth: Curtin University.

Wubbels, Th., & Brekelmans, M. (1998). The teacher factor in the social climate of the classroom. In B. J. Fraser & K. G. Tobin (Eds.), *International handbook of science education* (pp. 565–580). Dordrecht: Kluwer Academic Publishers.

Wubbels, Th., & Brekelmans, M. (2012). Teacher–students relationships in the classroom. In B. J. Fraser, K. G. Tobin, & C. J. McRobbie (Eds.), *Second international handbook of science education* (pp. 1241–1255). New York, NY: Springer.

Wubbels, Th., Brekelmans, M., den Brok, P., Levy, J., Mainhard, T., & van Tartwijk, J. (2012). Let's make things better: Developments in research on interpersonal relationships in education. In Th. Wubbels, P. den Brok, J. van Tartwijk, & J. Levy (Eds.), *Interpersonal relationships in education: An overview of contemporary research*

(Advances in Learning Environments Research Series) (pp. 225–250). Rotterdam, The Netherlands: Sense Publishers.

Wubbels, Th., Brekelmans, M., den Brok, P., Wijsman, L., Mainhard, T., & van Tartwijk, J. (2014). Teacher–student relationships and classroom management. In E. T. Emmer & E. J. Sabornie (Eds.), *Handbook of classroom management* (2nd ed., pp. 363–386). London: Routledge.

Wubbels, Th., Brekelmans, M., & Hooymayers, H. (1993). Comparison of teachers' and students' perceptions of interpersonal teacher behavior. In Th. Wubbels & J. Levy (Eds.), *Do you know what you look like* (pp. 64–80). London: Falmer Press.

Wubbels, Th., Brekelmans, M., Mainhard, T., den Brok, P., & van Tartwijk, J. (2016). Teacher-student relationships and student achievement. In K. R. Wentzel & G. B. Ramani (Eds.), *Handbook of social influences in school contexts: Social-emotional, motivation, and cognitive outcomes* (pp. 127–142). New York, NY: Routlegde.

Wubbels, Th., Créton, H. A., & Holvast, A. J. C. D. (1988). Undesirable classroom situations: A systems communication perspective. *Interchange, 19*(2), 25–40.

Wubbels, Th., Créton, H. A., & Hooymayers, H. P. (1985, April). *Discipline problems of beginning teachers: Interactional teacher behavior mapped out.* Paper presented at the Annual Meeting of the American Educational Research Association, Chicago, IL.

Wubbels, Th., Créton, H. A., & Hooymayers, H. P. (1987). A school-based teacher induction programme. *European Journal of Teacher Education, 10*, 81–94.

Wubbels, Th., Créton, H. A., Hooymayers, H. P., & Holvast, A. J. C. D. (1982). Training teachers to cope with the reality shock. *Studies in Science Education, 9*, 147–160.

Wubbels, Th., & Levy, J. (1991). A comparison of interpersonal behavior of Dutch and American teachers. *International Journal on Intercultural Relationships, 15*(1), 1–18.

Zijlstra, H., Wubbels, Th., Brekelmans, M., & Koomen, H. M. Y. (2013). Child perceptions of teacher interpersonal behavior and associations with mathematics achievement in Dutch early grade classrooms. *The Elementary School Journal, 113*(4), 517–540.

CHAPTER 3

Developments in Quantitative Methods and Analyses for Studying Learning Environments

Perry den Brok
Wageningen University, Wageningen, The Netherlands

Tim Mainhard
Utrecht University, Utrecht, The Netherlands

Theo Wubbels
Utrecht University, Utrecht, The Netherlands

1   Introduction

Since the 1980s, the domain of learning environments has shown considerable growth, in terms of both topics of study and methods used to study learning environments. In the first issue of the first volume of the journal *Learning Environments Research*, Fraser (1998a, p. 7) introduced this research as follows:

> In the 30 years since the pioneering use of classroom environment assessments in an evaluation of Harvard Project Physics (Walberg & Anderson, 1968), the field of learning environments has undergone remarkable growth, diversification and internationalisation. Several literature reviews (Fraser, 1986, 1994, 1998b; Fraser & Walberg, 1991) place these developments into historical perspective and show that learning environment assessments have been used as a source of dependent and independent variables in a rich variety of research applications spanning many countries. The assessment of learning environments and research applications have involved a variety of quantitative and qualitative methods, and an important accomplishment within the field has been the productive combination of quantitative and qualitative research methods.

The present chapter summarizes developments in research methods and analyses used in research on learning environments. This description is largely based on studies reported in the seminal journal in this area, *Learning*

Environments Research (published by Springer), and the book series, *Advances in Learning Environments Research* (published by Brill Sense), even though we take occasional steps outside these outlets by referring to handbooks or studies on learning environments published elsewhere.

In several literature reviews, Fraser (1998b, 2007, 2012, 2014) identifies the types of past research on learning environments: (1) associations between student outcomes and the environment, (2) evaluation of educational innovations, (3) differences between students' and teachers' perceptions of the same environment, (4) combining qualitative and quantitative methods, (5) determinants of learning environment perceptions and (6) cross-national and multicultural studies. This overview shows that the methods used in learning environments research have undergone impressive changes from more descriptive and evaluative approaches to more explanatory, predictive and model-testing ones, and that researchers have employed a variety of methods to investigate issues related to learning environments.

Quantitative methods and analyses formed the starting point, are still used in many studies of learning environments and are our own primary area of expertise. In line with this expertise, we focus in this chapter on developments that have taken place in *quantitative* methods and those in which we largely have been involved. By choosing this focus, in no way, do we want to imply that qualitative methods are not important or valuable. On the contrary, qualitative methods are, for example, often needed to provide deeper and more detailed insights into the more-general trends and associations that quantitative methods can provide and which often can be used to explain *how and why* things happen.

With respect to quantitative approaches certainly in the initial phases of learning environments research, many studies have been conducted to develop and validate instruments to map various dimensions of the learning environment, mostly via questionnaires assessing the perceptions of students and/or teachers over a series of lessons or learning activities (Fraser, 1986, 1994, 1998b, 2007). In these questionnaires, groups of items build scales, and the scales can be classified, for example, in terms of the dimensions of Moos (1974, 1979) for classifying human environments. Moos distinguishes Relationship dimensions, (which identify the nature and intensity of personal relationships and assess the extent to which people are involved in the environment and support and help each other), Personal Development dimensions (which assess personal growth and self-enhancement as a focus of the learning environment) and System Maintenance and System Change dimensions (which involve the extent to which the environment is orderly, clear in expectations, maintains control and is responsive to change). Questionnaires most commonly used in learning environments research include: the Learning Environment Inventory (LEI); Classroom Environment Scale (CES); Individualised Classroom Environment Questionnaire (ICEQ); My Class Inventory (MCI); College and University Classroom Environment Inventory (CUCEI); Questionnaire on Teacher Interaction (QTI); Science Laboratory Environment Inventory (SLEI); Constructivist Learning Environment Survey (CLES); and the What Is Happening In this Class? (WIHIC) questionnaire (Fraser, 2012, 2014).

We characterise in this chapter the development of quantitative research methods in the domain of learning environments research roughly in two phases and provide a future perspective. The first phase constitutes the early decades (1965–2000), in which the main foci of research were to establish reliable and valid instruments for mapping various dimensions and indicators of the learning environment, to establish links with variables that might help to constitute the learning environment perceptions, to investigate links with learning outcomes, and to identify differences in perceptions between major groups of respondents, such as between genders, grade levels or ethnic groups. The emphasis of much research in this phase was descriptive or correlational. The second phase roughly constitutes the period between 2000 and the present, when many learning environments researchers started using advanced statistical techniques such as multilevel analysis or structural equation modeling and when more varied research questions were investigated, leading to a diversity of methods used. The next phase will be the (near) future; even though it is unclear what the future will bring, the latest developments in educational research highlight the use of large data (e.g., learning analytics), the use of analysis methods such as modeling, simulation, network analyses, probability analyses and data analytics, and further development of existing statistical methods and techniques. We elaborate each period in more detail in the following sections.

2   Early Years (1965–2000): Descriptive and Correlational Research

During the early years of learning environments research, researchers mainly focused on the first type (linking perceptions to outcomes), third type (differences between teacher and student perceptions) and fifth type (linking environments and environment dimensions) types of research as distinguished by Fraser (1998b).

With respect to establishing the quality of questionnaires and measurement instruments, researchers used a variety of analysis methods (e.g. Fraser, 1998b; see also Westerhof & de Jong, 2002). Typically, these involved establishing each scale's internal consistency (e.g. alpha reliability coefficient) and discriminant validity (e.g. using the mean correlation of a scale with the other scales in the same instrument as a convenient index), and the ability of a scale to differentiate between the perceptions of students in different classrooms (significance level and eta squared statistic from ANOVAs). With respect to these indicators, it became clear that most instruments were able to produce scales with Cronbach's alphas above 0.70, that most learning environment instruments were able to distinguish between classes to some degree (eta squared values ranging between 0.10 and 0.25 on average; with the QTI as an outlier with eta squared values between 0.25 and 0.50), and that instruments were able to differentiate between different factors or dimensions in the learning environment (correlations between scales often ranging between 0.20 and 0.60, indicating some overlap and an idiosyncratic measurement). In addition, item and scale orderings were investigated via exploratory factor analyses in which factor loadings were used to see to what degree items could be linked to their supposed constructs. Most of the earlier mentioned instruments were able to find and replicate consistent factor loading patterns, with items loading most strongly on their expected scales (e.g. loadings larger than 0.40) and weakly on other scales.

Furthermore, researchers used descriptive analyses and analyses of variance to indicate to what degree students or teachers experienced certain dimensions of the learning environment and to what degree there were differences in perceptions according to background characteristics of respondents or their classes and teachers. Researchers for example[1] focused on differences between teacher and student perceptions (Fisher & Fraser, 1983; Fraser, 2007; den Brok, Bergen, & Brekelmans, 2006), between genders (Doppelt, 2004; Ferguson & Fraser, 1999; Henderson, Fisher, & Fraser, 2000; Huang, 2003; Levy, den Brok, Wubbels, & Brekelmans, 2003; Waxman & Huang, 1998), between different ages or grade levels (Levy et al., 2003; Waxman & Huang, 1998), between ethnic groups (Aldridge & Fraser, 2000; den Brok & Levy, 2005) or between other variables describing background characteristics of respondents. These studies reported that, in many cases, girls had more favourable perceptions of the learning environment than boys, that students from lower grade levels had higher scores for perceptions of learning environment dimensions than students from higher grade levels, and that considerable differences existed between different countries or ethnic groups in terms of their perceptions of the learning environment.

To establish associations between perceptions and learning outcomes – particularly cognitive and affective outcomes, such as subject-related attitudes – researchers mainly conducted correlational analyses (to obtain bivariate associations) or regression analyses (to obtain multivariate associations corrected for other variables) (e.g. den Brok, Brekelmans, & Wubbels, 2004; Fraser & Fisher, 1983; Goh & Fraser, 1998; Kim, Fisher, & Fraser, 2000; Wong & Fraser, 1996). Typically, regression analyses indicated weaker associations than bivariate correlations because of the overlap between predictors. With such regression analyses, researchers were also able to detect the unique and overlapping contributions of different dimensions of the learning environment to the association with student outcomes, for example by including both the relationship dimension and the system maintenance and change dimension. Results generally have indicated that dimensions and scales often overlap in their associations with outcomes but that, despite such overlap, still considerable unique effects still can be found for single dimensions or scales.

3 Methodological Diversification (2000–Present)

In the second period, many of the methods used previously continued to be in use. However, partly because of new software and statistical developments and partly because of critiques of earlier methods, the second period can be characterised by diversification in the use of quantitative methods and analyses. A few trends can be seen, as discussed below.

The first and maybe most fundamental change is the use of *multilevel analyses*. Many learning environment studies collect perception data from entire classes and from multiple classes within schools. As such, data-points are not independent, but data are hierarchical in nature, with students nested in classes, classes nested under teachers, and teachers nested in schools. For example, it can be argued (and it has been shown many times) that the perceptions of students in the same class or taught by the same teacher in a certain school are likely to be more similar compared with those of students or teachers in other classes or schools (Hox, 2002; Snijders & Bosker, 1999). However, traditional analyses of variance or regression analyses do not take this into account, leading to inaccurate and often overestimated associations between variables (Dorman, 2009; Lüdtke, Trautwein, Kunter, & Baumert, 2006). In addition, background variables that affect perceptions also can exist at different levels or exert different effects at different levels; for example, grade level is a characteristic of all students in a class, while student gender is an individual student-level variable. Although the first multilevel analyses in educational research date back to the second part of the twentieth century (e.g., Brekelmans, 1989), it is only since the beginning of the new millennium that easy accessible software and analysis methods were developed to take this hierarchical structure into account and to study the effect of factors at their actual level of measurement. As a result, several researchers started (and continue) to use such multilevel methods to investigate the effect of background variables on perceptions of the learning environment, or to investigate the associations between learning environments and student outcomes (Allodi, 2002; den Brok, Brekelmans, & Wubbels, 2006; Dorman, Kennedy, & Young, 2015; Levy et al., 2003; Maulana, Opdenakker, den Brok, & Bosker, 2012; Pinger, Rakoczy, Besser, & Klieme, 2017; Young, 2000; Webster & Fisher, 2003). These studies showed that indeed the effects of variables in past studies were often overestimated, and that it is particularly hard to explain individual differences in student perceptions, compared with differences between classes or teachers (Levy et al., 2003; Maulana et al., 2012). Interestingly, the studies also showed that student characteristics can be differently associated with outcomes or perceptions at the individual level and at higher levels, such as the classroom. For example, it was found that not only individual student gender was associated with perceptions of the learning environment, but also the percentage of boys or girls in the classroom (Levy et al., 2003). A similar finding was reported with respect to student ethnicity (den Brok & Levy, 2005).

Another development during this period was the use of *structural equation modelling* in learning environments research. In structural equation models, observed variables (often questionnaire items) can be linked to their latent constructs (often 'scales' or 'dimensions') and associations between these latent constructs can be established. Structural equation models also allow researchers to model chains of associations between variables, thereby allowing for testing both direct as well as indirect (statistical) effects (Back, Polk, Keys, & McMahon, 2016; Johnson & Stevens, 2006; Mok, 2002). In this respect, structural equation modeling allows testing theories or expected causal mechanisms (structural relations) and the structure of items into factors or dimensions (Kong, 2008; Nitz, Prechtl, & Nerdel, 2014). Furthermore, structural equation modeling even allows distinguishing between groups and testing a causal mechanism or model across different groups, to see if it upholds for these different groups. When combining multilevel analyses with structural equation modeling, we enter the field of multilevel structural modelling. Such combined models at this moment allow for models at not more than 2 levels. Of course, combinations of all of the aforementioned are also possible, such as multi-group multi-level models. Learning environments researchers started to use SEM to conduct so-called confirmatory factor analyses to test a particular factor structure (often the hypothesised factor structure of their instrument). For example, researchers using the QTI used this method to test whether items were ordered in terms of the eight sectors of interpersonal behaviour and if these sectors (or items) were ordered in a circular or so-called circumplex structures (den Brok et al., 2006; Sivan, Cohen, Chan, & Kwan, 2017; Sun, Mainhard, & Wubbles, 2017). Given the circular ordering of the constructs, the researchers were able to test not only specific relations, but even specific expected factor loadings. This way, more rigorous tests of construct validity could be conducted than in the past, providing further evidence to support or detract from the quality of the instruments. In a different fashion, structural models have been used to establish mechanisms or chains of associations of learning environment variables to other variables. Den Brok and colleagues (den Brok, Wubbels, van Tartwijk, & Veldman, 2010) tested a model in which teacher interpersonal behaviour was linked to student outcomes in different ethnic groups in their Dutch sample. With these analyses, they were able to show that interpersonal behaviour was related to these outcomes in a much different way for Turkish and Morrocan students than for Dutch-born students, and that the associations of such behaviour with outcomes were also larger for the former than for the latter group.

A third important development was the use of *Rasch models* to study learning environment instruments. In Rasch analyses, questionnaire items that are assumed to be linked to one dimension, such as a particular teaching competence or the degree to which the classroom environment can be regarded as constructivist. Furthermore, it is assumed that certain items are less applicable to some persons than to others (e.g. the degree to which a teacher uses ICT in the classroom) and therefore they can be argued to have a higher 'difficulty' of occurring in reality. With Rasch analyses, it can be tested whether certain items or scales can be ordered under a higher-order dimension and whether certain scales (or items) are more common to be applicable than others. It allows ordering both respondents and items on the same dimension: items in terms of difficulty or likelihood to apply for any respondent and respondents for their 'true' score on the dimension based on measurement of all items. Several studies have been reported in the *Learning Environments Research* journal using this approach (e.g. Cavanagh, 2015; Cavanagh & Romanoski, 2006; Cavanagh & Waugh, 2011; Dymnicki, Henry, & Myford, 2015; Maulana & Helms-Lorenz, 2016; Niklas, Nguyen, Cloney, Taylor, & Adams, 2016; Peoples, O'Dwyer, Wang, Brown, & Rosca, 2014; Waugh & Cavanagh, 2002). Maulana and Helms-Lorenz (2016), for example, in their study of students' perceptions of teaching, found that teacher behaviours concerning the clarity of their instruction and their provision of a learning climate were most commonly perceived, followed by activating instruction and classroom management, and with adaptive instruction or differentiation of teaching-learning strategies as the least common behaviours perceived by students in the classroom. Typically, these less-frequently occurring behaviours can be considered 'more difficult' and results from analyses such as these can thus be used to structure curricula or to train teachers.

A fourth development as of 2000 was the use of more *person-centred approaches* to analysis rather than variable-centred approaches. In person-centred approaches, the idea is to distinguish between different groups of respondents (e.g. types of students) based on how they 'score' on different learning environment variables. This way, typologies can be constructed. If such typologies can be enriched with more qualitative descriptions and labels, this could enhance their recognisability or help people to reflect on them or become more aware (Rickards, den Brok, & Fisher, 2005). Also the interpretation of, for example, the effects certain environment variables on individuals can be interpreted with more ease. In the Netherlands, Brekelmans (1989) was one of the first to use cluster analysis to construct a typology of teachers' interpersonal behaviour. She distinguished between eight types or teacher profiles – directive, authoritative, tolerant/authoritative, tolerant, uncertain/tolerant, uncertain/aggressive, repressive and drudging – and these profiles also were later established in other countries such as Australia (Fisher, den Brok, Waldrip, & Dorman, 2011; Rickards et al., 2005). Profiles have also been constructed using other instruments, such as the WIHIC (den Brok, Telli, Cakiroglu, Taconis, & Tekkaya, 2010; Giallousi, Giamalas, & Pavlatou, 2013). In the WIHIC study, den Brok et al. (2010) found six distinct classroom environment profiles: the self-directed learning classroom, the task-oriented cooperative learning classroom, the mainstream classroom, the task-oriented individualised classroom, the low-effective classroom and the high-effective classroom. In some studies, profiles have been linked to student outcomes. More recently, structural equation modeling has been combined with profile analyses, leading to latent profile analysis (Schenke, Ruzek, Lam, Karabenick, & Eccles, 2017; Seidel, 2006). Latent profile analysis is more precise for constructing typologies because measurement errors and background characteristics of respondents can be taken into account during the analyses.

In a fifth and final development, a small set of studies involved collecting longitudinal data and used multilevel analyses of variance to investigate developments in perceptions of the learning environment, via so-called *growth curve analyses* (e.g. Davis, Chang, Andrzejewski, & Poirier, 2014). For teacher interpersonal behaviour, researchers have reported developments in perceptions during the teaching career or during the course of the year (Wubbels, Brekelmans, den Brok, & van Tartwijk, 2006; Mainhard, Brekelman, den Brok, & Wubbels, 2011). These studies showed that different dimensions or aspects can develop differently. Agency or influence, for example, showed a steep increase during the first ten years of the career, after which a period of stability began, with a gradual decrease during the final years of the career. Proximity or communion, on the other hand, showed a slow but gradual decline during the career. Over the course of a year, both influence and proximity showed a curvilinear development, first with a small decrease and then with an increase towards the end of the year. The higher initial influence/proximity was the less pronounced than the decrease was.

4   Future Developments

Several developments that started during the last ten years are likely to be continued now and in the upcoming years. For example, multilevel analysis and structural equation modeling are becoming more mainstream and integrated with each other and are even considered the standard for studies in which data are collected in a hierarchical fashion. More and more complex models with direct and mediating effects are being used and also, for longitudinal data, these models are being tested. For example, in a cross-lagged panel design, variables are measured at different points in time. Thus, the effect of a variable (e.g. teacher strictness) on another variable (e.g. student motivation) can be investigated and, at the same time, compared with the reciprocal effects of, in this example, student motivation on teacher strictness. As a result of such developments, research is getting more precise in what and how factors affect the perceptions of students and teachers of the learning environment, to what degree and via what mechanisms. Thus, more precision is gained in establishing how learning environment variables affect student outcomes. Researchers more often include multiple variables in their analyses, rather than studying or analysing a single variable at a time.

Of course, methodological developments do not come to a halt. New and exciting developments are already in sight. A first observation that can be made is that there is a need for more *theory development* in learning environments research. These theories should concern the relations between different concepts, between different dimensions of the learning environment and between learning environment aspects and learning outcomes. Theory development is needed from a methodological perspective because analysis methods described in the previous section are less exploratory and descriptive, and more based on assumptions or hypotheses to be tested. For example, structural equation models require firm theoretical frameworks because, in practice, an infinite number of models can be tested against the data and even multiple models can hold, even if some, theoretically, make more sense than others. Bayesian statistics, which also are becoming more mainstream, assume certain relationships between variables, and depart on the basis of testing against probability. In a different fashion, analyses methods such as Rasch or multilevel analyses require variables to display certain characteristics, such as normality. Currently, many studies and instruments are more based on an empirical basis (picking a set of variables to see which turn up as relevant or are statistically associated with outcomes), rather than a theoretical basis.

Typically, much of the quantitative research on learning environments has concentrated on more stable and long-term perceptions. However, little is known about how perceptions are formed or developed, and how specific events or experiences lead to certain perceptions. *Moment-to-moment data* collected in the learning environment are more often collected in a different fashion, for example, via speech/text analysis (Song & McNary, 2016), Qualitative Comparative Analysis (Nijssen, Hillebrand, de Jong, & Kemp, 2012), observation systems using joy-stick coding (Pennings, van Tartwijk, Wubbels, Claessens, van der Want, & Brekelmans, 2014) or eye-trackers (Van den Bogert, Van Bruggen, Kostons, & Jochems, 2014; Wolff, Jarodzka, van den Bogert, & Boshuizen, 2016; McIntyre, Mainhard, & Klassen, 2017), etc. Current developments in ICT, such as learning management systems or other systems that generate so-called big data, allow different types of datasets to be collected. To analyse such data and to link them to the more long-term perception data brings new methodological challenges, such as sequential analyses (Furtak, Araceli Ruiz-Primo, & Bakeman, 2017), probabilistic analyses, etc. They also require new ways to report and interpret data, such as via visualisations (e.g., Mainhard, Pennings, Wubbels, & Brekelmans, 2012) and simulations. In this respect, it might be fruitful for learning environment researchers to connect with scholars from other domains, such as statisticians, mathematicians, software engineers and psychologists, and to open themselves for new frameworks. A good example is the advancement of dynamic systems theory and chaos theory. These theories specifically aim to search for patterns in seemingly chaotic data, link trends at different time frames, and allow other than linear relationships between variables. To analyse moment-to-moment interactions in the class and to link these to perceptions of teacher–student interpersonal behaviour, for example, Pennings and colleagues used state-space grids (Pennings & Mainhard, 2016; Pennings et al., 2014) and time-line charts (Pennings, Brekelmans, Wubbels, van der Want, Claessens, & van Tartwijk, 2014). These methods show how developments occur over time (on a plane or linear graph) and how they can be related to more-general perceptions.

Pennings, for example, found that a teacher with an uncertain/aggressive profile, compared with a teacher with a tolerant/authoritative profile, showed much more variation on a state-space grid in real-time interactions with students. This means that certain profiles in teaching can become visible in small changes in moment-to-moment interactions. Yet another method is orbital decomposition (Guastello, Peressini, & Bond, 2011; Pincus, Ortega, & Metten, 2010), in which text or other data are analysed for recurring patterns of events in time series data. Such analyses can show if certain events reoccur in seemingly chaotic data and, if so, how much time elapses between these reoccurrences.

A third development relates to the *types of learning environments* investigated. More and more, learning environments research moves beyond the borders of the classroom and includes out-of-school learning environments or informal learning environments (Tal, 2001), such as museums (Holmes, 2011; Andre, Durksen, & Volman, 2017; Bamberger, 2009), field trips (Rebar, 2012), and outreach activities (Vennix, den Brok, & Taconis, 2017; Zaragoza & Fraser, 2017). Also, researchers extend their research from psychosocial factors (such as those mentioned by Moos, 1974) to physical factors, such as tools and materials involved, classroom spaces and school building characteristics (Cleveland & Fisher, 2014; Fisher, 2016; Imms, Cleveland & Fisher, 2016; Liu, Zandvliet, & Hou, 2012; Mäkelä & Helfenstein, 2016; Nidzam Che Ahmad, Osman, & Halim, 2013; Zandvliet & Broekhuizen, 2017; Zandvliet & Fraser, 2005). Moving beyond these traditional borders will require new types of data collection, such as real-time observations of space use and positioning of respondents, as well as physical measurement of aspects such as sound, light and air quality. To map transitions between in-class and out-of-class environments, still other data collection methods might be needed, such as analysis of email, tweets, contributions to online discussions (Song & McNary, 2011) or network surveys (Heldens, Bakx, & den Brok, 2016). These again could lead to the use of different types of analysis tools, such as word cloud instruments, network analysis software and text analysis software.

5 Conclusion

In sum, not only has learning environments research shown an incredible development in the use of quantitative methods from more-traditional descriptive, correlational and variance analytic approaches to more model testing, confirmatory, multilevel and other advanced techniques, but it also seems that learning environments research still has exciting times ahead as an evolving field of research, in terms of foci, concepts and theories and data-collection and data-analysis methods.

Note

1 The studies mentioned here are only examples, as there have been many studies published during this period; which makes it impossible to mention all of them.

References

Aldridge, J. M., & Fraser, B. J. (2000). A cross-cultural study of classroom learning environments in Taiwan and Australia. *Learning Environments Research, 3*, 101–134.
Allodi, M. W. (2002). A two-level analysis of classroom climate in relation to social context, group composition, and organization of special support. *Learning Environments Research, 5*, 253–274.
Andre, L., Durksen, T., & Volman, M. L. (2017). Museums as avenues of learning for children: A decade of research. *Learning Environments Research, 20*, 47–76.
Back, L. T., Polk, E., Keys, C. B., & McMahon, S. D. (2016). Classroom management, school staff relations, school climate, and academic achievement: Testing a model with urban high schools. *Learning Environments Research, 19*(3), 397–410.
Bamberger, Y., & Tal, T. (2009). The learning environment of natural history museums: Multiple ways to capture students' views. *Learning Environments Research, 12*, 115–129.
Brekelmans, M. (1989). *Interpersonal teacher behaviour in the classroom* [in Dutch]. Utrecht: WCC.
Cavanagh, R. F. (2015). A unified model of student engagement in classroom learning and classroom learning environment: One measure and one underlying construct. *Learning Environments Research, 18*, 349–361.
Cavanagh, R. F., & Romanoski, J. T. (2006). Rating scale instruments and measurement. *Learning Environments Research, 9*, 273–289.
Cavanagh, R. F., & Waugh, R. F. (Eds.). (2011). *Applications of Rasch measurement in learning environments research* (Advances in Learning Environments Research Series). Rotterdam, The Netherlands: Sense Publishers.
Cleveland, B., & Fisher, K. (2013). The evaluation of physical learning environments: A critical review of the literature. *Learning Environments Research, 17*, 1–28.
Davis, H., Chang, M. L., Andrzejewski, C. E., & Poirier, R. R. (2014). Examining relational engagement across the transition to high schools in three US high

schools reformed to improve relationship quality. *Learning Environments Research, 17,* 263–286.

den Brok, P., Brekelmans, M., & Wubbels, Th. (2004). Interpersonal teacher behavior and student outcomes. *School Effectiveness & School Improvement, 15,* 407–442.

den Brok, P., Brekelmans, M., & Wubbels, Th. (2006). Multilevel issues in research using students' perceptions of learning environments: The case of the questionnaire on teacher interaction. *Learning Environments Research, 9,* 199–213.

den Brok, P., Telli, S., Cakiroglu, J., Taconis, R., & Tekkaya, C. (2010). Learning environment profiles of Turkish secondary biology classrooms. *Learning Environments Research, 13,* 187–204.

den Brok, P. J., Bergen, T. C. M., & Brekelmans, J. M. G. (2006). Convergence and divergence between students' and teachers' perceptions of instructional behaviour in Dutch secondary education. In M. S. Khine & D. L. Fisher (Eds.), *Contemporary approaches to research on learning environments: World views* (pp. 125–160). Singapore: World Scientific.

den Brok, P. J., & Levy, J. (2005). Teacher-student relationships in multicultural classes: Reviewing the past, preparing the future. *International Journal of Educational Research, 43*(1–2), 72–88.

den Brok, P. J., Wubbels, Th., Veldman, I. M. J., & van Tartwijk, J. W. F. (2010). The differential effect of the teacher-student interpersonal relationship on student outcomes for students with different ethnic backgrounds. *British Journal of Educational Psychology, 80*(2), 199–221.

Doppelt, Y. (2004). Impact of science-technology learning environment characteristics on learning outcomes: Pupils' perceptions and gender differences. *Learning Environments Research, 7*(3), 271–293.

Dorman, J. P. (2009). Statistical tests conducted with school environment data: The effect of teachers being clustered within schools. *Learning Environments Research, 12*(2), 85–99.

Dorman, J., Kennedy, J., & Young, J. (2015). The development, validation and use of the Rural and Remote Teaching, Working, Living and Learning Environment Survey (RRTWLLES). *Learning Environments Research, 18,* 15–32.

Dymnicki, A. B., Henry, D. B., & Myford, C. M. (2015). The development of an instrument to measure school readiness for a prevention program. *Learning Environments Research, 18,* 267–287.

Ferguson, P. D., & Fraser, B. J. (1999). Changes in learning environments during the transition from primary to secondary school. *Learning Environments Research, 1,* 369–383.

Fisher, D. L., den Brok, P., Waldrip, B., & Dorman, J. (2011). Interpersonal behavior styles of primary education teachers during science lessons. *Learning Environments Research, 14,* 187–204.

Fisher, D. L., & Fraser, B. J. (1983). A comparison of actual and preferred classroom environments as perceived by science teachers and students. *Journal of Research in Science Teaching, 20*, 55–61.

Fisher, K. (Ed.). (2016). *The translational design of schools: An evidence-based approach to aligning pedagogy and learning environments* (Advances in Learning Environments Research Series). Rotterdam, The Netherlands: Sense Publishers.

Fraser, B. J. (1986). *Classroom environment*. London: Croom Helm.

Fraser, B. J. (1994). Research on classroom and school climate. In D. Gabel (Ed.), *Handbook of research on science teaching and learning* (pp. 493–541). New York, NY: Macmillan.

Fraser, B. J. (1998a). Classroom environment instruments: Development, validity and applications. *Learning Environments Research, 1*(1), 7–33.

Fraser, B. J. (1998b). Science learning environments: Assessment, effects and determinants. In B. J. Fraser & K. G. Tobin (Eds.), *International handbook of science education* (pp. 527–564). Dordrecht: Kluwer.

Fraser, B. J. (2007). Classroom learning environments. In S. K. Abell & N. G. Lederman (Eds.), *Handbook of research on science teaching* (pp. 103–124). Mahwah, NJ: Lawrence Erlbaum Associates.

Fraser, B. J. (2012). Classroom learning environments: Retrospect, context and prospect. In B. J. Fraser, K. G. Tobin, & C. J. McRobbie (Eds.), *Second international handbook of science education* (pp. 1191–1239). New York, NY: Springer.

Fraser, B. J. (2014). Classroom learning environments: Historical and contemporary perspectives. In N. Lederman & S. Abell (Eds.), *Handbook of research on science education volume II* (pp. 104–119). New York, NY: Routledge.

Fraser, B. J., & Fisher, D. L. (1986). Predicting students' outcomes from their perceptions of classroom psychosocial environment. *American Educational Research, 19*, 498–518.

Fraser, B. J., & Walberg, H. J. (Eds.). (1991). *Educational environments: Evaluation, antecedents and consequences*. London: Pergamon.

Furtak, E. M., Araceli Ruiz-Primo, M., & Bakeman, R. (2017). Exploring the utility of sequential analysis in studying informal formative assessment practices. *Educational Measurement, 36*(1), 28–38.

Giallusi, M., Gialamas, V., & Pavlatou, E. A. (2013). A typology of chemistry classroom environments: Exploring the relationships between 10th grade students' perceptions, attitudes and gender. *Learning Environments Research, 16*, 349–366.

Goh, S. C., & Fraser, B. J. (1998). Teacher interpersonal behavior, classroom environment and student outcomes in primary mathematics in Singapore. *Learning Environments Research, 1*, 199–229.

Guastello, S. J., Peressini, A. F., & Bond, R. W. (2011). Orbital decomposition for ill-behaved event-sequences: Transients and superordinate structures. *Nonlinear Dynamics, Psychology, and Life Sciences, 15*, 465–476.

Heldens, H., Bakx, A., & den Brok, P. (2016). Teacher educators' collaboration in subject departments: Collaborative activities and social relations. *Educational Research and Evaluation, 21,* 515–536.

Henderson, D., Fisher, D., & Fraser, B. J. (2000). Interpersonal behavior, laboratory learning environments and student outcomes in senior biology classes. *Journal of Research in Science Teaching, 37*(1), 26–43.

Holmes, J. A. (2011). Informal learning: Student achievement and motivation in science through museum-based learning. *Learning Environments Research, 14,* 263–277.

Hox, J. J. (2002). *Multilevel analysis: Techniques and applications.* Mahwah, NJ: Lawrence Erlbaum Associates.

Huang, S. Y. L. (2003). Antecedents to psychosocial learning environments in middle school classrooms in Taiwan. *Learning Environments Research, 6*(2), 119–135.

Imms, W., Cleveland, B., & Fisher, K. (Eds.). (2016). *Evaluating learning environments: Snapshots of emerging issues, methods and knowledge* (Advances in Learning Environments Research series). Rotterdam, The Netherlands: Sense Publishers.

Johnson, B., & Stevens, J. J. (2006). Student achievement and elementary teachers' perceptions of school climate. *Learning Environments Research, 9*(2), 111–122.

Kim, H. B., Fisher, D. L., & Fraser, B. J. (2000). Classroom environment and teacher interpersonal behavior in secondary science classes in Korea. *Evaluation and Research in Education, 14*(1), 3–22.

Kong, C. K. (2008). Classroom learning experiences and students' perceptions of quality of school life. *Learning Environments Research, 11*(2), 111–129.

Levy, J., den Brok, P., Wubbels, Th., & Brekelmans, M. (2003). Students' perceptions of the interpersonal aspect of the learning environment. *Learning Environments Research, 6,* 5–36.

Liu, C. J., Zandvliet, D., & Hou, I. L. (2012). The learning environment associated with information technology in Taiwan: Combining psychosocial and physical aspects. *Learning Environments Research, 15,* 379–402.

Lüdtke, O., Trautwein, U., Kunter, M., & Baumert, J. (2006). Reliability and agreement of student ratings of the classroom environment: A reanalysis of TIMSS data. *Learning Environments Research, 9,* 215–230.

Mainhard, M. T., Brekelmans, M., den Brok, P., & Wubbels, Th. (2011). The development of the classroom social climate during the first months of the school year. *Contemporary Educational Psychology, 36,* 190–200.

Mainhard, M. T., Pennings, H. J., Wubbels, Th., & Brekelmans, M. (2012). Mapping control and affiliation in teacher–student interaction with state space grids. *Teaching and Teacher Education, 28*(7), 1027–1037.

Mäkelä, T., & Helfenstein, S. (2016). Developing a conceptual framework for participatory design of psychosocial and physical learning environments. *Learning Environments Research, 19,* 411–440.

Maulana, R., & Helms-Lorenz, M. (2016). Observations and student perceptions of the quality of pre-service teachers' teaching behaviour: Construct representation and predictive quality. *Learning Environments Research, 19*, 335–357.

Maulana, R., Opdenakker, M. C., den Brok, P., & Bosker, R. (2012). Teacher-student interpersonal relationships in Indonesian lower secondary education: Teacher and student perceptions. *Learning Environments Research, 15*, 251–271.

McIntyre, N. A., Mainhard, M. T., & Klassen, R. M. (2017). Are you looking to teach? Cultural, temporal and dynamic insights into expert teacher gaze. *Learning and Instruction, 49*, 41–53.

Mok, M. M. C. (2002). Determinants of students' quality of school life: A path model. *Learning Environments Research, 5*, 275–300.

Moos, R. H. (1974). *The social climate scales: An overview*. Palo Alto, CA: Consulting Psychologists Press.

Moos, R. H. (1979). *Evaluating educational environments: Procedures, measures, findings and policy implications*. San Francisco, CA: Jossey-Bass.

Nidzam Che Ahmad, C., Osman, K., & Halim, L. (2013). Physical and psychosocial aspects of the learning environment in the science laboratory and their relationship to teacher satisfaction. *Learning Environments Research, 16*, 367–385.

Nijssen, E. J., Hillebrand, B., de Jong, J. P. J., & Kemp, R. G. M. (2012). Strategic value assessment and explorative learning opportunities with customers. *Journal of Product Innovation Management, 29*, 91–102.

Niklas, F., Nguyen, C., Cloney, D. S., Taylor, C., & Adams, R. (2016). Self-report measures of the home learning environment in large scale research: Measurement properties and associations with key developmental outcomes. *Learning Environments Research, 19*(2), 181–202.

Nitz, S., Prechtl, H., & Nerdel, C. (2014). Survey of classroom use of representations: Development, field test and multilevel analysis. *Learning Environments Research, 17*, 401–422.

Pennings, H. J. M., Brekelmans, M., Wubbels, Th., van der Want, A. C., Claessens, L. C. A., & van Tartwijk, J. (2014). A nonlinear dynamical systems approach to real-time teacher behavior: Differences between teachers. *Nonlinear Dynamics, Psychology, and Life Sciences, 18*(1), 23–45.

Pennings, H. J. M., & Mainhard, T. (2016). Analyzing teacher-student interactions with state space grids. In M. Koopmans & D. Stamovlasis (Eds.), *Complex dynamical systems in education: Concepts, methods and applications* (pp. 233–271). New York, NY: Springer.

Pennings, H. J. M., van Tartwijk, J., Wubbels, Th., Claessens, L. C. A., van der Want, A. C., & Brekelmans, M. (2014). Real-time teacher-student interactions: A dynamic systems approach. *Teaching and Teacher Education, 37*, 183–193.

Peoples, S. M., O'Dwyer, L. M., Wang, Y., Brown, J. J., & Rosca, C. V. (2014). Development and application of the Elementary School Science Classroom Environment Scale (ESSCES): Measuring students' perceptions of the constructivism in the science classroom. *Learning Environments Research, 17,* 49–73.

Pincus, D., Ortega, D. L., & Metten, A. M. (2010). Orbital decomposition for multiple time series comparisons. In S. J. Guastello & R. A. M. Gregson (Eds.), *Nonlinear dynamical systems analysis for the behavioral sciences using real data.* Boca Raton, FL: CRC Press.

Pinger, P., Rakoczy, K., Besser, M., & Klieme, E. (2017). Interplay of formative assessment and instructional quality: Interactive effects on students' mathematics achievement. *Learning Environments Research, 20,* 1–19.

Rebar, B. M. (2012). Teachers' sources of knowledge for field trip practices. *Learning Environments Research, 15,* 81–102.

Rickards, T., den Brok, P., & Fisher, D. L. (2005). The Australian science teacher: A typology of teacher-student interpersonal behaviour in Australian science classes. *Learning Environments Research, 8,* 267–287.

Schenke, K., Ruzek, E., Lam, A. C., Karabenick, S., & Eccles, J. (2017). Heterogeneity of student perceptions of the classroom climate: A latent profile approach. *Learning Environments Research, 20,* 289–306.

Seidel, T. (2006). The role of student characteristics in studying micro teaching learning environments. *Learning Environments Research, 9,* 253–271.

Sivan, A., Cohen, A., Chan, D. W. K., & Kwan, Y. W. (2017). The circumplex model of the questionnaire on teacher interaction among Hong Kong students: A multidimensional scaling solution. *Learning Environments Research, 20,* 189–198.

Snijders, T. A. B., & Bosker, R. J. (1999). *Multilevel analysis.* London: Sage Publications.

Song, L., & McNary, S. (2011). Understanding students' online interaction: Analysis of discussion board postings. *Journal of Interactive Online Learning, 10*(1), 1–14.

Sun, X., Mainhard, T., & Wubbels, Th. (2017). Development and evaluation of a Chinese version of the Questionnaire on Teacher Interaction (QTI). *Learning Environments Research, 21*(1), 1–17.

Tal, R. T. (2001). Incorporating field trips as science learning environment enrichment: An interpretive study. *Learning Environments Research, 4,* 25–49.

Tobin, K., & Fraser, B. J. (1998). Qualitative and quantitative landscapes of classroom learning environments. In B. J. Fraser & K. G. Tobin (Eds.), *International handbook of science education* (pp. 623–640). Dordrecht: Kluwer.

van den Bogert, N., van Bruggen, J., Kostons, D., & Jochems, W. M. G. (2014). First steps into understanding teachers' visual perception of classroom events. *Teaching and Teacher Education, 37*(1), 208–216.

Vennix, J., den Brok, P., & Taconis, R. (2017). Perceptions of STEM-based outreach learning activities in secondary education. *Learning Environments Research, 20*, 21–46.

Walberg, H. J., & Anderson, G. J. (1968). Classroom climate and individual learning. *Journal of Educational Psychology, 59*, 414–419.

Waugh, R. F., & Cavanagh, R. F. (2002). Measuring parent receptivity towards the classroom environment using a Rasch measurement model. *Learning Environments Research, 5*, 329–352.

Waxman, H. C., & Huang, S. L. (1998). Classroom learning environments in urban elementary, middle, and high schools. *Learning Environments Research, 1*, 95–113.

Webster, B. J., & Fisher, D. L. (2003). School-level environment and student outcomes in mathematics. *Learning Environments Research, 6*(3), 309–326.

Westerhof, K. J., & de Jong, R. (2002). The quality of student ratings of teacher behaviour. *Learning Environments Research, 4*, 51–85.

Wolff, C. E., Jarodzka, H., van den Bogert, N., & Boshuizen, E. (2016). Teacher vision: Expert and novice teachers' perception of problematic classroom management scenes. *Instructional Science, 44*, 243–265.

Wong, A. L. F., & Fraser, B. J. (1996). Environment–attitude associations in the chemistry laboratory classroom. *Research in Science and Technological Education, 14*, 91–102.

Wubbels, Th., Brekelmans, M., den Brok, P., & van Tartwijk, J. (2006). An interpersonal perspective on classroom management in secondary classrooms in the Netherlands. In C. Evertson & C. S. Weinstein (Eds.), *Handbook of classroom management: Research, practice and contemporary issues* (pp. 1161–1191). New York, NY: Lawrence Erlbaum Associates.

Young, D. (2000). Teacher morale in Western Australia: A multilevel model. *Learning Environments Research, 3*, 159–177.

Zandvliet, D., & Broekhuizen, A. (2017). Spaces for learning: Development and validation of the school physical and campus environment survey. *Learning Environments Research, 20*, 175–187.

Zandvliet, D. B., & Fraser, B. J. (2005). Physical and psychosocial environments associated with networked classrooms. *Learning Environments Research, 8*, 1–17.

Zaragoza, J. M., & Fraser, B. J. (2017). Field-study science classrooms as positive and enjoyable learning environments. *Learning Environments Research, 20*(1), 1–20.

CHAPTER 4

Looking Back and Looking Forward

David B. Zandvliet
Simon Fraser University, Burnaby, Canada

As noted at the beginning of this book, this edited volume is a commemorative work celebrating the Special Interest Group on Learning Environments (SIG 120) of the American Educational Research Association. My involvement with this group has been as the Elected Chair over the last few years and, together with SIG co-founder (Barry Fraser), we proposed and co-edited this book to commemorate the SIG's 30th anniversary. As such, the structure and format of the book have been designed to look back on the past 30 years to document how the research developed over time and to identify the major themes that dominated the research agenda over this timeframe. A second task was to highlight contemporary learning environment studies as they are now being undertaken.

1   Looking Back

Barry Fraser (Curtin University, Australia) began this historical perspective in Chapter 1 by recounting the formation of the Learning Environments SIG in 1984 and its first program space at the AERA annual meeting in Chicago in 1985. He also described how actions taken at that time contributed to the SIG's ultimate success, expansion and internationalisation. This retrospective on psychosocial learning environments also noted other historical landmarks in the development of the field, such as the creation of the international journal *Learning Environments Research*.

Theo Wubbels (Utrecht University, the Netherlands) described 30 years of research on learning environments from an interpersonal perspective in Chapter 2. His research program demonstrates that good interpersonal relationships between teacher and students are key to high-quality learning environments. Studying learning environments from an interpersonal perspective, with a focus on teacher–student relationships, shows that that teacher–student relationships are related to student outcomes and that they can develop and change over the span of a teaching career.

Den Brok and colleagues (also from the Netherlands) continued with a historical perspective by summarising important developments in research methods and methods of statistical analysis used in research on learning environments in Chapter 3. They characterise the development of (largely) quantitative research methods in two phases. First, in the 'early decades' (1965–2000), the main foci of research were establishing reliable and valid instruments for mapping dimensions of the learning environment, investigating links between learning environment and student outcomes, and identifying differences in perceptions among genders, grade levels, ethnic groups, etc. They emphasised that much of the research then was descriptive or correlational in nature. They also described a second phase (2000 to the present) when many researchers began using more-advanced statistical techniques (such as multilevel analysis or structural equation modeling) and when more varied research questions were being investigated, leading to a greater diversity in research methods.

2   Early Conceptions

As confirmed by its history, the study of learning environments currently remains a thriving field within educational research. The conceptual framework for the study of learning environments is rooted in the work of Kurt Lewin, Henry Murray, Herbert Walberg, and Rudolf Moos (Fraser, 1998). Early on, Lewin's (1951) field theory stipulated the key idea of learning environment research, namely, that human behaviour has two determinants: the environment and its interaction with an individual's personal characteristics. To illustrate this, Lewin (1936) created the formula $B = f(P, E)$ in which behaviour is a function of both the person and the environment.

Murray (1938) developed a theory to describe a person's needs and the environment. He defined needs as those that are the specific, innate and personal requirements for an individual, such as personal goals. An individual's need to achieve these goals, or drive to attain them, is an important factor in an individual's personality. Factors that were considered beyond an individual's control, that could either enhance or limit that individual's achievement of personal goals (or needs), were defined by Murray as *press*. Murray used *alpha press* to refer to an external observer's perceptions of the learning environment and *beta press* to refer to observations by the constituent members of the environment under observation (Murray, 1938).

Stern, Stein, and Bloom (1956) built on Murray's (1938) work by subdividing beta press into the individual perception of the environment that each student holds versus a shared view that the students hold collectively as a group about the learning environment. They used *private beta press* to represent the idiosyncratic view that an individual student has of a classroom environment and *consensual beta press* for the shared view of the students' perceptions. Learning environment researchers often utilise consensual beta press for data collected through survey and observation methods and private beta press for interviews or focus groups conducted with respondents.

Over the ensuing decades, a wide range of research instruments have been constructed, tested and validated to describe psychosocial learning environments. This started with the Classroom Environment Scale (CES, Moos, 1974, 1979) and the Learning Environment Inventory (LEI) developed for Harvard Project Physics by Walberg and Anderson (1968). In several comprehensive literature reviews, Fraser (1994, 1998, 2007, 2014) identified various types of past research on learning environments including: (1) associations between student outcomes and the environment, (2) evaluation of educational innovations (e.g. Spinner & Fraser, 2005), (3) differences between students' and teachers' perceptions of the same environment, (4) combining qualitative and quantitative methods, (5) determinants of learning environment perceptions, (6) cross-national and multicultural studies and (7) action research aimed at improving classrooms (e.g. Fraser, 1981).

3   Affordances of the Methodology

Because learning is no longer viewed as an individualised phenomenon for much of educational research, the learning environments approach has continually stressed over time that studying the achievement of individual students has limited value, because learning occurs within and under the strong influence of social factors (Fraser, 2007, 2014). Importantly, studies during the past few decades have also diversified to involve the use of qualitative methods in describing psychosocial learning environments (e.g. Anstine Templeton & Nyberg, 1997) and the combination of both qualitative and quantitative methods (e.g. Aldridge, Fraser, & Huang, 1999; Anstine Templeton & Johnson, 1998; Fraser & Tobin, 1991; Tobin & Fraser, 1998).

Today, learning environments research has diversified and various approaches, studies and instruments have been developed, tested and validated in diverse settings and countries, with particular attention to science education contexts (Fraser, 1998, 2014). This research trajectory has also "provided convincing evidence that the quality of the classroom environment in schools is a significant determinant of student learning" (Dorman, Fisher, & Waldrip, 2006, p. 2). Further, there remains compelling evidence to suggest that classroom environments of various types can have a strong effect on other types of student outcomes including attitudes (Fraser & Butts, 1982; Fisher & Khine, 2006; Fraser, 2007, 2014; Fraser & Walberg, 1991).

Major dimensions of learning environments include classroom relationships, system maintenance and change, and (personal) growth (Moos, 1979). Historically, the major dimensions that differentiate different types of learning environments are (1) learning goals, (2) division of learner and teacher roles and (3) the roles of learners in relation to each other. For example, learning outcomes can be categorised into cognitive, affective or metacognitive domains; divisions between teachers and students can range from more teacher-centred to more student-centred; and environments can be more focused on individual learning versus more collaborative learning.

For me, a key element in learning environment research lies in its ability to predict positive student learning outcomes. This in turn underscores a continuing need to develop exemplary methods to measure, map or typify various types of learning environments. In this, contemporary research combines a variety of information sources and can utilise both qualitative and quantitative data sources. Most often, learning environment research makes use of the perceptions of those involved in the learning environment (e.g. teachers, students, parents, administrators) in addition to other methods (such as classroom observation or document analysis). These can help us to make distinctions between perceptions of the actual learning environment and those of preferred or desired learning environments as envisioned by today's students (Fraser, 2007, 2014).

Perhaps, most importantly, learning environment research can give a voice to both students and teachers in demonstrating what is effective in the classroom, regardless of the subject area or disciplinary context. Put simply, students' perceptions about their educational experiences are an invaluable resource for understanding the complexity of today's learning environments (Fraser, 1991, 1998, 2014). Ideally these would be complemented by observation, interview or other rich sources of qualitative data.

4   Contemporary Learning Environments

In the broadest perspective, the concept of a learning environment today not only includes the psychosocial dimensions already described above (Fraser, 2007, 2014), but also includes the physical structure and set-up of schools, classes or institutions (Zandvliet, 2012). Further, learning environments have other antecedents (conditions, input) that influence the learning outcomes of both students and teachers (Fraser, 1998), Hence, lesson materials, an increasingly 'technological' curriculum and teachers variations in practice (as mediated by expertise, knowledge and behaviour) also are integral to the description of contemporary learning environments.

Early in my career, I developed what I termed an 'ecological' framework for this broader conceptualisation of a learning environment. In part, the model responded to what I described as a 'technologising' of curriculum that is still evident in the current waves of STEM or STEAM Education which are influencing the newest models of curriculum reform in science, mathematics and other curriculum areas worldwide. The model (Figure 4.1) makes explicit this influence of physical space as an important component of this broader learning environment.

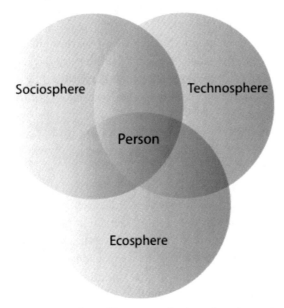

FIGURE 4.1   Ecological factors contributing to learning environments

Reframing our conception of a learning environment (or revisiting its original premise) can guide researchers in thinking about factors that drive change in today's increasingly complex educational settings. The model described in Figure 4.1 consists of three spheres of influence, namely, the *ecosphere*, *sociosphere* and *technosphere* which are all considered to be interrelated components of a more holistic view of the learning environment. *Ecosphere* refers simply to a person or group's physicality and surroundings (physical learning environment), while *sociosphere* relates to an individual's net interactions with people within that environment (psychosocial learning environment). Finally, *technosphere* is the total of all tools and techniques (person-made things). In educational environments, this last factor is created and deeply influenced by teachers' practice. In a holistic sense, the model describes all influences that act on individuals and groups in today's increasingly diverse learning environments.

We can relate this model back to the metaphor of a 'traditional' classroom. The *ecosphere* refers to the physical spaces (indoors and out) that make up the learning space. This model considers those influences under the notion of *ecology*, but this environment can contain 'natural' and/or 'built' elements. The *sociosphere* refers to our interrelationship with other people over time that occur within these learning spaces. These factors are considered as aspects of the psychosocial learning environment and relate closely to earlier views about classroom learning environments. Lastly, the *technosphere* refers to the remaining 'tools' and 'teaching practices' occurring in the learning environment according to those who 'inhabit' them. Of course, these factors should not be considered alone because they make up a complex ecology. This ecology applies to a diverse array of learning environments whether they are traditional classrooms, outdoor learning spaces or other technology-infused 'places' for learning and teaching.

5 New Physical Contexts

There is now widespread acceptance that the teaching and learning landscape in schools is rapidly evolving, therefore requiring educators to employ increasingly innovative approaches to ensure that students stay engaged with learning (Kuhlthau et al., 2015). As educators rethink their teaching practices and employ more student-centred approaches, the traditional layouts of classrooms (typified by rows of desks and chairs) no longer lend themselves to progressive practices taking place within them (Byers et al., 2014; Fisher, 2010, 2016).

The integration of virtual spaces into the teaching and learning environment further necessitates changes to classroom design (Chandra & Mills, 2015; Zandvliet & Fraser, 2005). This point has led to many improvements in the design of learning spaces to allow for dynamic teaching and learning (Cleveland & Fisher, 2014).

For the purposes of much of this research, learning environments consist conceptually of both social and physical dimensions. For example, Hodgson (2002) measured physical factors but did not attempt to relate them to either the psychosocial environment or student outcomes. Horne Martin (2002) and Kennedy, Hodson, Dillon, Edgett, Lamb, and Rempel (2006) measured both classroom physical parameters and teacher activities and perceptions within the classroom space. Further research by Evans (2006) focused on factors within the physical environment (including behavioural toxicology, noise and crowding in relation to how they influence child development) as well as socio-emotional, cognitive, motivational and psycho-physiological outcomes. Finally, student perceptions of the classroom environment (Holley & Steiner, 2005) have also been linked to student perceptions of what and how much they learn.

Parallel to inherent changes in teachers' practices, there is a growing body of research documenting the strengthening relationship between the built learning environment and student outcomes (Blackmore et al., 2011). When effectively designed, physical learning environments (similar to psychosocial environments) have been found to facilitate constructivist pedagogy and student engagement (Cleveland, 2016). Gifford's (2002) analysis of the impact of the environment in educational settings revealed that space and how it is arranged have implications for student performance, with more-open environments having a positive effect on learning outcomes. Classroom aesthetics also can have a favourable influence on student perceptions of the learning environment (Zandvliet & Broekhuizen, 2017).

In a several studies of the physical environment of classrooms (e.g. Zandvliet & Broekhuizen, 2017; Zandvliet & Fraser, 2005), changes made to the design of contemporary learning environments encompassed a combination of physical, pedagogical and social contexts. As schools begin to shift to more student-centred approaches, traditional classroom configurations often inhibit teachers from teaching how they wish, and so teachers begin to adapt the physical classroom environment to better suit them. Changes to physical contexts range from removing rows of desks and chairs or replacing them with other furniture (such as couches, ottomans, beanbags, standing desks and coffee tables) to structural changes (such as open, collaborative learning spaces or smaller informal areas for quiet work). In a recent study involving the validation of a physical learning environment survey, Zandvliet and Broekhuizen (2017) determined that school architectural features, ambient factors (such as air quality), spatial and visual environments of the school, and features such as scale and aesthetics in buildings are important in students' perceptions of the learning environment.

Importantly, the physicality of the learning environment is not limited simply to the school campus or its classrooms. As a new model of 21st Century Learning is increasingly reflected in curriculum reform efforts worldwide, there is a corresponding focus on community as an appropriate parallel location for teaching and learning (outside formal school settings). This development is reflected in the increasing amount of research literature devoted to 'context-based' forms of education (e.g. context-based science curriculum) and in a resurgence of interest in various forms of critical and place-based forms of education (Gruenewald, 2003). For example, in a recent study of learning environment in 'place-based education' settings (Zandvliet, 2012), constructs such as 'community engagement' and 'environmental interaction' were important aspects of the learning environment. This point seems to underscore the fact that the physical contexts for schooling are changing rapidly from both within and without traditional classrooms.

6   Looking Forward

Until only recently, learning environment studies concentrated mainly on narrower science and technology education milieus, but these methods are increasingly being viewed as applicable to inter/multi-disciplinary fields of study, such as place-based forms of education and other disciplines such as English (Lim & Fraser, in press). By studying the learning environment as perceived by student participants, the types of environments that promote positive environmental attitudes, achievement and other desirable social attributes in students could eventually be described. The remainder of this book is intended to highlight several case studies of learning environments research that give an indication of where the field could be heading in its new-found diversity both within and outside of the constraints of science education.

In this chapter, it has been my task to describe several of these new areas of promise for learning environments research that include new and diverse contexts or applications. While these include established research programs in areas such as information and communications technology or place-based education, they also include emerging research contexts such as physical classroom environments and links among learning environment variables and other student outcomes. Of additional interest to me in this exploration of possible futures is the potential link between learning environments research and the literature on student engagement (as just one example).

The concept of school engagement is attracting increasing attention as representing a solution to declining academic motivation and achievement among students and it is likely to be closely related to students' perceptions about the learning environment. Engagement is presumed to be malleable, responsive to contextual features and (similar to learning environments) amenable to environmental change. Researchers have described behavioural, emotional and cognitive forms of engagement and they often study engagement as a multifaceted construct (Fredricks et al., 2004). For me, the potential contribution of this concept to learning environments research has yet to be fully realised. This suggests that, by increasing the repertoire of research methods, we might come up with even richer characterisations of how students feel, think and behave. Looking forward, such future research could aid in the development of finely-tuned interventions for a wide variety of learning environments in both K-12 and post-secondary settings.

7 Remaining Chapters

In Chapter 5, Catherine Martin-Dunlop and colleagues (Morgan State University, USA) describe research into the link between an enriched classroom design and active learning in a senior-level university architecture course. The conception of the learning environment in this study relates closely to the model of *ecosphere* described earlier in this chapter. In this study, two classes of students served as the control group (n_1=29) and received their instruction in a traditional seminar-style classroom. Two classes served as the experimental group (n_2=20), had the same instructor and syllabus, and completed the same activities and projects. Cognitive and affective outcomes were assessed throughout the study and included students' perceptions of the enriched versus the traditional classroom learning environment, enjoyment of lessons, academic self-efficacy, comparisons of predicted and actual final grades, and quantification of students' movements and interactions in both sets of classes. Student surveys, focus-group interviews, instructor interviews, instructor journals and videotape analyses of all lessons comprised the data-collection methods. Findings included statistically-significant increases in student-to-student interactions, as well as higher average item means for 3 out of 12 learning environment scales (Physical Space, Material Environment, Innovation) in the designed, active learning environment relative to the traditional classroom environment. Also, achievement scores for the course were higher in the active learning classroom. This research provides a case study of how the physical environment of classrooms can influence the overall learning environment and student achievement.

In Chapter 6, Georgeos Sirrakos (Kutztown University, USA) and Barry Fraser describe the development and validation of the Questionnaire Assessing Connections to Science (QuACS). This survey assesses students' perceptions of their learning environment, their attitudes toward science, and their engagement with new approaches to delivering college physics content through narratives and place-based learning opportunities. Therefore, this study relates closely to aspects of the *technosphere* in the model in Figure 4.1

because different pedagogical techniques were modified to gauge the impact on the overall learning environment. When the QuACS was field-tested with a sample of 495 undergraduate students, data analyses supported the factor structure and internal consistency reliability of six scales included in this survey (Personal Relevance, Innovation, Future Intentions to Study Science, Self-Efficacy in Science, Scientific Storytelling, and Place-based Learning). This study demonstrates how the learning environment of a classroom can be augmented by a variety of social and pedagogical factors which, in turn, potentially can impact on other outcomes such as student attitudes, self-efficacy and engagement.

In Chapter 7, David Henderson and Melissa Loh (Rossmoyne Senior High School, Australia) report a mixed-methods study in which students' classroom environment perceptions guided a program of teacher professional learning at a senior high school in Western Australia. This chapter is relevant to how teachers' practice influences the overall learning environment, especially the *technosphere* in the model of learning environments described earlier in Figure 4.1. The high-school teacher professional learning program involved a range of disciplines and the integration of feedback from students' perceptions of their classroom learning environment using the Classroom Climate Questionnaire (CCQ) with teachers' feedback from a classroom observation program. Participating teachers used feedback from these two sources in devising intervention strategies in their endeavour to optimise the classroom learning environment in their courses. Feedback from the classroom observations provided teachers with a highly-valued source of data that complemented data from the school's well-established CCQ-based program in supporting teacher professional learning. The chapter provides a case study of how teachers can effectively use an action research agenda using learning environment instruments to guide their own efforts in improving pedagogy and to further take control of their own professional development.

In Chapter 8, Alisa Stanton, David Zandvliet and Rosie Dhaliwahl (Simon Fraser University, Canada) describe aspects of a collaborative research program involving a health promotion unit at a Canadian university and academic researchers. The study's purpose was to ascertain the impact of learning environments on student well-being within a higher-education setting. Several psychosocial scales from the What Is Happening In this Class? (WIHIC) and Place-based Learning and Constructivist Environment Survey (PLACES) were adapted for use in a new instrument. Also included were measures of well-being, including the PANAS affective well-being scale, a 'Flourishing' scale and a single item measuring Life Satisfaction. Surveys were administered to 842 undergraduate students in 13 classes in the faculties of Health Sciences,

Science & Arts and Social Sciences. Initial results suggest a relationship between students' experiences of learning environments and students' well-being outcomes. Because students in higher education are reported as experiencing negative well-being outcomes at increasingly-high levels today, it is important to consider whether creating positive conditions for well-being in postsecondary learning environments could provide an avenue for supporting student well-being more broadly within and across post-secondary institutions. This study indicates yet another possible type of student outcome associated with the learning environment of students, namely, the promotion of sustained psychological well-being.

References

Aldridge, J. M., Fraser, B. J., & Haung, T. (1999). Investigating classroom environments in Taiwan and Australia with multiple research methods. *Journal of Educational Research, 93*, 48–57.

Anstine Templeton, R., & Johnson, C. E. (1998). Making the school environment safe: Red Rose's formula. *Learning Environments Research, 1*, 35–57.

Anstine Templeton, R., & Nyberg, L. (1997). Making sense of it all: Using science to teach at risk students how to succeed. In D. L. Fisher & T. Rickards (Eds.), *Science, mathematics and technology education and national development: Proceedings of the 1997 international conference on science mathematics and technology education, January, 1997, Hanoi, Vietnam* (pp. 329–336). Perth: Curtin University of Technology.

Blackmore, J., Bateman, D., Loughlin, J., O'Mara, J., & Aranda, G. (2011). *Research into the connection between built learning spaces and student outcomes.* Melbourne: Department of Education and Early Childhood Development.

Byers, T., Imms, W., & Hartnell-Young, E. (2014). Making the case for space: The effect of learning spaces on teaching and learning. *Curriculum and Teaching, 29*(1), 5–19. doi:10.7459/ct/29.1.02

Chandra, V., & Mills, K. A. (2015). Transforming the core business of teaching and learning in classrooms through ICT. *Technology, Pedagogy and Education, 24*(3), 285–301.

Cleveland, B. (2016). Addressing the spatial to catalyse socio-pedagogical reform in middle years education. In K. Fisher (Ed.), *The translational design of schools: An evidence-based approach to aligning pedagogy and learning environments* (pp. 27–50). Rotterdam, The Netherlands: Sense Publishers.

Cleveland, B., & Fisher, K. (2014). The evaluation of physical learning environments: A critical review of the literature. *Learning Environments Research, 17*(1), 1–28.

Dorman, J. P., Fisher, D. L., & Waldrip, B. G. (2006). Learning environments, attitudes, efficacy and perceptions of assessment: A LISREL analysis. In D. L. Fisher & M. S. Khine (Eds.), *Contemporary approaches to research on learning environments: Worldviews* (pp. 1–28). Singapore: World Scientific.

Evans, G. W. (2006). Child development and the physical environment. *Annual Review of Psychology, 57*, 423–451.

Fisher, D. L., & Khine, M. (Eds.). (2006). *Contemporary approaches to research on learning environments: Worldviews*. Singapore: World Scientific Publishing.

Fisher, K. D. (2010). *Technology-enabled active learning environments: An appraisal*. Paris: OECD Publishing.

Fisher, K. D. (Ed.). (2016). *The translational design of schools: An evidence-based approach to aligning pedagogy and learning environments*. Rotterdam, The Netherlands: Sense Publishers.

Fraser, B. J. (1981). Using environmental assessments to make better classrooms. *Journal of Curriculum Studies, 13*(2), 131–144.

Fraser, B. J. (1991). Two decades of classroom environment research. In B. J. Fraser & H. J. Walberg (Eds.), *Educational environments: Evaluation, antecedents and consequences* (pp. 3–27). London: Pergamon Press.

Fraser, B. J. (1994). Research on classroom and school climate. In D. Gabel (Ed.), *Handbook of research on science teaching and learning* (pp. 493–541). New York, NY: Macmillan.

Fraser, B. J. (1998). Science learning environments: Assessment, effects and determinants. In B. J. Fraser & K. G. Tobin (Eds.), *International handbook of science education* (pp. 527–564). Dordrecht: Kluwer.

Fraser, B. J. (2007). Classroom learning environments. In S. K. Abell & N. G. Lederman (Eds.), *Handbook of research on science education* (pp. 103–125). London: Routledge.

Fraser, B. J. (2014). Classroom learning environments: Historical and contemporary perspectives. In N. Lederman & S. Abell (Eds.), *Handbook of research on science education* (Vol. II, pp. 104–119). New York, NY: Routledge.

Fraser. B. J., & Butts, W. L. (1982). Relationship between perceived levels of classroom individualization and science-related attitudes. *Journal of Research in Science Teaching, 19*(2), 143–154.

Fraser, B. J., & Tobin, K. (1991). Combining qualitative and quantitative methods in classroom environment research. In B. J. Fraser & H. J. Walberg (Eds.), *Educational environments: Evaluation, antecedents and consequences* (pp. 271–292). London: Pergamon Press.

Fraser, B. J., & Walberg, H. J. (Eds.). (1991). *Educational environments: Evaluation, antecedents and consequences*. Oxford: Pergamon Press.

Fredricks, J. A., Blumenfeld, P. C., & Paris, A. H. (2004). School engagement: Potential of the concept, state of the evidence. *Review of Education Research, 74*(1), 59–109.

Gifford, R. (2002). *Environmental psychology: Principles and practice.* Colville, WA: Optimal Books.

Gruenewald, D. (2003). The best of both worlds: A critical pedagogy of place. *Educational Researcher, 32*(4), 3–12.

Holley, L. C., & Steiner, S. (2005). Safe space: Student perspectives on classroom environment. *Journal of Social Work Education, 41,* 49–64.

Horne Martin, S. (2002). The classroom environment and its effects on the practice of teachers. *Journal of Environmental Psychology, 22,* 139–156.

Kennedy, S. M., Hodgson, M., Dillon Edgett, L., Lamb, N., & Rempel, R. (2006). Subjective assessment of listening environments in university classrooms: Perceptions of students. *Journal of the Acoustical Society of America, 119,* 299–309.

Kuhlthau, C. C., Maniotes, L. K., & Caspari, A. K. (2015). *Guided inquiry: Learning in the 21st century* (2nd ed.). Westport, CT: Greenwood.

Lewin, K. (1936). *Principles of topological psychology.* New York, NY: McGraw.

Lewin, K. (1951). *Field theory in social science: Selected theoretical papers* (D. Cartwright, Ed.). New York, NY: Harper & Row.

Lim, C.-T. D., & Fraser, B. J. (in press). Learning environments research in English classrooms. *Learning Environments Research.*

Moos, R. H. (1974). *The social climate scales: An overview.* Palo Alto, CA: Consulting Psychologists Press.

Moos, R. H. (1979). *Evaluating educational environments.* San Francisco, CA: Jossey-Bass.

Murray, H. A. (1938). *Explorations in personality.* New York, NY: Oxford University Press.

Spinner, H., & Fraser, B. J. (2005). Evaluation of an innovative mathematics program in terms of classroom environment, student attitudes, and conceptual development. *International Journal of Science and Mathematics Education, 3,* 267–293.

Stern, G., Stein, M., & Bloom, B. (1956). *Methods in personality assessment.* Glencoe, IL: The Free Press.

Tobin, K., & Fraser, B. J. (1998). Qualitative and quantitative landscapes of classroom learning environments. In B. J. Fraser & K. G. Tobin (Eds.), *International handbook of science education* (pp. 623–640). Dordrecht: Kluwer.

Walberg, H. J., & Anderson, G. J. (1968). Classroom climate and individual learning. *Journal of Educational Psychology, 59*(6), 414–419.

Zandvliet, D. B. (2012). Development and validation of the Place-based Learning and Constructivist Environment Survey (PLACES). *Learning Environments Research, 15*(1), 125–140.

Zandvliet, D. B., & Broekhuizen, A. (2017). SPACES for learning: Development and validation of the school physical and campus environment survey. *Learning Environments Research, 20*(2), 174–187.

Zandvliet, D. B., & Fraser, B. (2005). Physical and psychosocial environments associated with Internet classrooms. *Learning Environments Research, 8*(1), 1–17.

CHAPTER 5

Evaluating the Impact of a Purposefully-Designed Active Learning Space on Student Outcomes and Behaviours in an Undergraduate Architecture Course

Catherine Martin-Dunlop
Morgan State University, Baltimore, Maryland, USA

Christine Hohmann
Morgan State University, Baltimore, Maryland, USA

Mary Anne Alabanza Akers
Morgan State University, Baltimore, Maryland, USA

Jim Determan
Hord Coplan Macht, Baltimore, Maryland, USA

LaKeisha Lewter
Morgan State University, Baltimore, Maryland, USA

Isaac Williams
Morgan State University, Baltimore, Maryland, USA

Architects say 'space matters'. Neurobiologists know that an enriched environment stimulates new synaptic networks between neurons leading to improved learning. And educators emphasise how variables can rarely be controlled in the messiness of teaching and learning environments. By blending these three different but complementary paradigms together as we did in this research, we produced a one-of-a-kind study that makes a unique contribution across several disciplinary fields. Our pilot study took place over two semesters in 2014 at Morgan State University, a Historically Black College/University (HBCU) in Baltimore, Maryland, USA, in an architecture course called Design and Human Behavior. This chapter describes the quasi-experimental study in which we investigated the link between an enriched classroom design created to promote active learning and improved student outcomes. We define active learning as any instructional method that engages students in the learning process (Prince, 2004). During active learning, higher-order/critical thinking, discussions and activities are the mainstay (Freeman et al., 2014). Students frequently work in collaborative groups, and are not merely passive recipients of information – which is often the case in a teacher-centred environment.

The study is distinctive for several reasons. In the field of learning environments research, it is the first known study to involve a transdisciplinary team of researchers as well as a racially/ethnically diverse group of students at a unique post-secondary institution (an HBCU). We feel that a transdisciplinary approach is necessary in order to tackle 21st century issues in education. The problem has been that "… researchers generally consider teaching and learning apart from the architectural setting …" (Gislason, 2010, p. 127). However, recently, "increasing numbers of both educators and design professionals are becoming aware of the important role that physical space plays in educational settings" (Cleveland & Fisher, 2014, p. 1). The study included the first known use of a behaviour recognition software program typically used in controlled biological experiments with rodents. The program codes organism-to-organism or organism-to-object interactions that have been video recorded, and we applied the same method with our undergraduate students. Thirdly, the Architecture Learning Environment Survey includes a new scale called Physical Space that assesses the extent to which a classroom space promotes effective learning. This emerging area of learning environments research in post-secondary institutions, that makes the 'design of space' the focus, promises to yield fruitful transdisciplinary studies that can provide an alternative lens for understanding the complexities of learning.

1 Background

1.1 *Moos' Three-Dimensional Model*

Questionnaires and surveys developed over the past 40 years have been used effectively to measure a host of variables that describe a typical classroom learning environment. Most of these instruments are based on Moos' three-dimensional scheme or model. Moos was the pioneer psychologist who paved the way for the fields of both learning environments and social or human ecology by studying places as diverse as psychiatric hospitals, university residences, conventional work sites, and correctional institutions such as prisons. Of practical concern in both fields was the question: How can an environment be created to maximise human functioning and competency? (Moos, 1979). Moos' studies eventually took him to educational settings, such as schools and classrooms, where the focus became how to create environments that promote effective student learning.

Even today, with learning environment instruments being translated into different languages, such as Spanish, Mandarin and Arabic, or being modified to meet unique situations (e.g., online and distance learning), researchers still attempt to cover two or three of Moos' categories from this social ecological perspective. The categories are based on Relationship, Personal Development, and System Maintenance and Change dimensions. However, Moos' third dimension, System Maintenance and Change, tends to be overlooked. What is noticeable within the learning environments research field is that only two instruments – the Learning Environment Inventory (LEI) (Fraser, Anderson, & Walberg, 1982; Walberg & Anderson, 1968) and the Science Laboratory Environment Inventory (SLEI) (Fraser, Giddings, & McRobbie, 1995) – include a scale (called Material Environment) assessing the *physical* environment that would fit under Moos' System Maintenance and Change. In the SLEI, Material Environment assesses the extent to which the laboratory equipment and materials are adequate. Five of seven items explicitly refer to physical attributes of a room. Interestingly, as other instruments came onto the learning environments research scene, scales were merged into new surveys to reflect more contemporary educational views as well as to create parsimony, Material Environment, seemed to slip by the wayside. Only relatively recently, thanks to researchers in architecture, urban planning and design (Cleveland & Fisher, 2014), and in educational technology, has a focus on how the physical learning environment or space affects student educational outcomes re-emerged.

1.2   Interest in Classroom Design and Learning Spaces

Studies of new classroom designs and their effect on student outcomes have been conducted across a range of disciplines at post-secondary institutions around the globe. Work at North Carolina State University (NCSU) and Massachusetts Institute of Technology (MIT) pioneered investigations of the impact of active learning classroom (ALC) designs in the US. Researchers with the Student-Centered Activities for Large Enrollment Undergraduate Programs project or SCALE-UP, that originated at NCSU, report that "over 50 schools across the country … have adopted it for classes of various sizes. SCALE-UP has also been employed in a variety of courses such as chemistry, biology, mathematics, engineering, and even comparative literature" (Gaffney et al., 2008, p. 48). Beichner et al. (2007) found that failure rates could be reduced to one-fifth of the rate in traditional classes among undergraduate physics students, particularly for women and minority students. Additionally, understanding of physics concepts improved as measured by the Force

Concept Inventory (the normalised gain was double that of a traditional lecture course and the best students showed the largest gain) (Hestenes, Wells, & Swackhamer, 1992). MIT's Technology Enabled Active Learning (TEAL) project, also with physics students, revealed the same results as NCSU when an active learning curriculum was used in the redesigned spaces (Dori & Belcher, 2005; Dori, Belcher, Besette, Danziger, McKinney, & Hult, 2003).

Researchers at the University of Minnesota (Brooks, 2011, 2012; Walker, Brooks, & Baepler, 2011; Whiteside, Brooks, & Walker, 2010) were the first to apply experimental controls in order to isolate the effect of learning space. During their initial pilot study, researchers were simply interested in gathering reactions to the campus' new, high-tech ALCs through interviews with students and faculty. An extension of this pilot study by Whiteside, Brooks, and Walker (2010) involved the effects of a large ALC and a traditional classroom more specifically on teaching and learning. Two sections of the same biology education course (N=86) took place in the two different environments. The researchers were able to establish a quasi-experimental design because most if not all variables were controlled in both settings, and only the physical space varied. By comparing students' American College Test (ACT) scores with their final course grades, the researchers found that students in the ALC exceeded expectations. This was because their average ACT score was significantly *lower* than the ACT scores of students in the traditional classroom but "... the average difference between the sections' final grades [was] statistically insignificant" (Whiteside, Brooks, & Walker, 2010, p. 7). Additionally, a classroom observation instrument covering 32 variables related to the classroom activities and behaviours of both an instructor and students was utilised. Five behaviours revealed statistically significant differences that favoured students in the ALC- less lecturing, more discussion, instructor at podium less, and more consulting. A test of statistical independence confirmed that these four behaviours were strongly correlated with classroom type (p<0.0001). Finally, a 5-scale student perception survey revealed statistically significant differences between the two learning spaces for four of the variables. Students in the ALC felt that the environment promoted engagement, enhanced their learning experiences (enrichment), provided flexibility in learning and was a good fit for the course.

A year later in 2011, University of Minnesota researchers replicated the above study (Brooks, 2012; Walker, Brooks, & Baepler, 2011) in a new building housing 10 additional ALCs, including one room that could hold up to 126 students. This time, they used a different instructor, student sample and course, and focused more on controlling pedagogy across the two classroom environments. In the large-enrollment freshmen biology course (N=263 split across the two rooms), again students in the ALC outperformed expectations when their ACT scores were compared with final course grades. Using the same classroom observation protocol, they also found that the biology instructor "... behaved differently in the two rooms" (Walker, Brooks, & Baepler, 2011, p. 7) even when most if not all variables were controlled and active learning was the goal in both classrooms.

It is often difficult in post-secondary institutions to conduct quasi-experimental studies of the effects of space on student outcomes. However, valuable work can still be accomplished and it must be acknowledged that different research designs have different purposes. Oblinger's edited book (2006) highlights additional post-secondary institutions that have created innovative learning spaces in business schools, libraries, science and mathematics classrooms, laboratory and technology centers, an auditorium, on-campus cafés, common areas and faculty training and student learning centres. Two recent edited books in the Advances in Learning Environments Research series provide numerous strategies for assessing and evaluating new types of learning spaces. Imms, Cleveland, and Fisher (2016) consider 13 different ways to assess innovative school designs, while Fisher (2016) uses an evidence-based, translational approach that originated in the health planning sector. Both edited books feature graduate students' dissertations from the University of Melbourne. Recently, an interest in developing new instruments that are valid and reliable to assess innovations in classroom design has emerged.

1.3   Development of New Instruments

Zandvliet (2014) developed and validated the Structural Physical and Campus Environment Survey (SPACES) with 160 pre-service teachers and their instructors in a post-secondary environmental education course in B.C., Canada. Participants completed a preferred form of SPACES to indicate what they would ideally like regarding structural, architectural and ambient features of their campus. Comparing participants' responses on a single, side-by-side form in which they can indicate what they prefer with what they actually experience is a common method used in learning environments research. However, Zandvliet only used a preferred version of his instrument. Participants chose options from a Likert scale ranging from 1 (Strongly Disagree) to 5 (Strongly Agree) to provide their perceptions of five physical constructs, each with five items – Spatial Environment, Scale and Esthetics, Ambient Factors, Architectural Elements, and Visual Environment. Participants' mean scores ranged from 4.37 to 4.57, and alpha reliability ranged from 0.68 for Scale and Esthetics to 0.84 for Visual Environment. Overall, this new instrument holds promise for future research on the evaluation of learning spaces in post-secondary environments.

Design researchers from the company, Steelcase Education Solutions (SES), worked closely with faculty from three universities to develop another survey. Scott-Webber, Strickland, and Ring Kapitula (2013) recognised that the role of the built environment is "... a variable often underemphasized ..." (p. 1) and wanted to find out if an intentionally-designed intervention affected student engagement. Their Active Learning Post-Occupancy Evaluation (AL-POE) has 12 factors/items that comprise the survey and cover Learning Practices and Solutions. The SES intentionally-designed spaces were known as Node Chairs®, LearnLab®, and Media:scape®, and involved 130 students and 17 faculty. Similar to comparing what students prefer with their actual perceptions of a learning environment using a single, side-by-side form, the AL-POE asked students to first compare their *old/pre* environment (what we call 'traditional') with their *new/post* environment during one administration. Response options consisted of 0 or 1 for Not OK to 2, 3 or 4 for OK. Internal reliability as measured by Cronbach's alpha was 0.91 for pre-Learning Practices, 0.93 for post-Learning Practices, 0.96 for pre-Solutions and 0.96 for post-Solutions. Overall, the researchers found that the differences for all 12 items on the Al-POE between the old/pre and the new/post classrooms were statistically significant ($p<0.0001$) in favour of the new SES spaces.

1.4 Context of the Pilot Study

This study took place at Morgan State University (MSU), a Historically Black College/University (HBCU) originally established in 1867 as the Centenary Biblical Institute. It is part of an American higher education system consisting of 107 two and four-year institutions nation-wide that receive federal funding, both public and private and including medical schools and law schools that were established prior to 1964. Historically, HBCUs' goal was to serve the African-American community when many Black students were denied attendance at traditionally White institutions. Nowadays, the percentage of Black students varies a great deal depending on the institution and state. In fact, several HBCUs have a very high population of White students (e.g., 85% at a college in West Virginia).

MSU is located in northeast Baltimore, Maryland, the largest of four HBCUs in the State. It is recognised as Maryland's primary public urban university that strives to address social, political and economic concerns among urban areas and underserved communities. Enrollment has been steady over the past five years (2011–2016) averaging a total of 7,787 students: 6,435 undergraduates and 1,352 graduate students. The overall racial/ethnic composition is 79.3% African-American, 8.7% international, 3.2% White, 3.3% multi-racial, 3.6% Hispanic, 0.8% Asian, 0.8% unknown, 0.2% Native American and 0.1% Native

Hawaiian (Fall 2016 figures). At MSU, there has been a concerted effort to diversify the student population and, hence, international students come from many countries including China, Nepal, Brazil, Saudi Arabia and several African countries, to name a few.

1.5 Purpose of Study

The purpose of this study was to evaluate the impact of a purposefully-designed, enriched, active learning environment on architecture students' outcomes and behaviors. The course involved in this study was an undergraduate course called Design and Human Behavior. This seminar-style course covers "the cultural, social, and psychological factors of human behavior that must be considered when exploring the built environment. Theories and methods of assessment and design are studied to understand the mutually supportive relationships between humans and their physical environments" (from course syllabus). Only one other known study involving architecture students' perceptions of their learning environment has been conducted in the past. Oluwatayo, Aderonmu, and Aduwo (2015) from Nigeria developed a new 36-item survey with a 1–5 Likert scale to assess perceptions of five variables among 273 students: the quality of instruction, academic atmosphere, friendship and student communities, student–lecturer interaction, and assessment. The authors concluded that "perceptions of the learning environment in architectural education are related to the space and effectiveness of the teaching process ..." (Oluwatayo, Aderonmu, & Aduwo, 2015, p. 139). However, the survey clearly did *not* assess students' perceptions of space. Only two items, ("I am satisfied with the size of my class and my classroom is organised" and "The facilities available in the classroom aid my learning") can be construed as possibly assessing students' opinions about the *physical* environment.

In our study, we intentionally manipulated the physical design of one of the two classrooms in which students would be undertaking their architecture course. Students in the experimental group had the course in the enriched, active learning classroom, while students in the control group had the course in a traditional-style classroom. Although similar past studies involved new school (Gislason, 2010) and post-secondary classroom designs (Beichner et al., 2007; Dori & Belcher, 2005; Gaffney et al., 2008; Scott-Webber, Strickland, & Ring Kapitula, 2013), only the University of Minnesota studies (Brooks, 2011, 2012; Walker, Brooks, & Baepler, 2011; Whiteside, Brooks, & Walker, 2010) controlled as many variables as we did in this pilot study. Additionally, our assessment strategies were extensive and contributed both breadth and depth to the resulting data.

2 Method

2.1 Participants

A total of 49 undergraduate students (the majority juniors/3rd year and seniors/4th year in a typical 4-year Bachelor's program) participated in the study during the two semesters of 2014. Their average age was 23.6 years. Most of the students were majoring in architecture and chose to enroll in the 15-week course, an elective within the School of Architecture and Planning. Twenty students (13 males and 7 females) were in the enriched, active learning classroom and 29 (17 males and 12 females) were in the traditional classroom. Students chose which class to be in based on their own personal schedule and, therefore, we could not randomly assign students to each class. Although Morgan State University is an HBCU and has 79.3% of students campus-wide who are Black or African American, our study's participants were unique in that they represented a wider range of races and ethnicities. Figure 5.1 illustrates the racial/ethnic make-up of the students.

Also, two male African-American instructors were involved in the study as participant observers. The spring 2014 instructor was an older man who had taught at the university for 11 years and then retired at the end of the semester. The fall 2014 instructor was considerably younger and worked as an adjunct (part-time) instructor because he was a full-time, practising architect at a large, international firm.

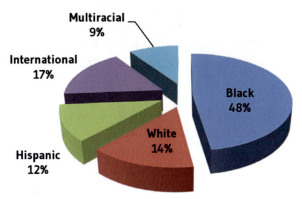

FIGURE 5.1 Racial/ethnic composition of undergraduate architecture students who participated in the study (N=49)

2.2 Research Design

The study used a quasi-experimental, mixed-method design that was evaluative in nature. Students in the traditional classroom (control group) had five long, stationary tables arranged horizontally with computers embedded in the tabletops and 4–5 standard chairs for each table, the lecturer's podium had a desktop computer, keyboard, LCD projector and student computer controls, and there was a large projection screen located at the front of the room. The instructor had control of the student computers but the computers were rarely used. One large whiteboard next to the door covered most of the front wall behind the screen.

The enriched, purposefully-designed active learning classroom had five round tables donated by Herman Miller, a 75-year-old and well-established office furniture company in the US. Tables and comfortable chairs were on wheels to allow for ease of movement. A wall-mounted, flat screen monitor controlled by a student's personal computer was located adjacent to each student group. Several large whiteboards were mounted on walls and smaller, mobile whiteboards were also available to students. There was no podium or obvious 'front of the room' for the instructor to stand and deliver information or lead class discussions.

Because both the experimental and control classrooms were roughly the same size, only the physical design of the two rooms varied as described above. All other variables, such as instructor, syllabus, course content, assigned readings, assessment strategies and time of day (9:30–10:50 am) were controlled. The control class met on Mondays and Wednesdays, and the experimental class met on Tuesdays and Thursdays. Importantly, the same instructor taught both sections of the course during the semester. Instructors were encouraged to teach using an active learning approach in *both* environments. Naturally, there were some differences between the two instructors, but both tried to maintain a consistent style across the two classroom settings.

2.3   Quantitative Data Collection

Methods included the use of a survey and videotape recordings of student behaviours in both the control and experimental classes. A comparison was made of students' final course grade with their accumulated grade point average (GPA) to generate a prediction of academic performance.

2.3.1   Survey

Scales from four valid and reliable learning environment instruments were used to create the Architecture Learning Environment Survey (ALES). Each scale contained five items that were selected by consensus among the researchers from items available in the original instrument. Table 5.1 provides for each instrument, the original developers' names, level of usage, the number of scales from the total available that were used, and how each scale is classified according to Moos' scheme described earlier.

What is most noteworthy about the ALES is that a new scale was created called Physical Space to satisfy the unique focus of the study on the physical attributes of a learning environment. Physical Space fits under Moos' dimension of System Maintenance and Change. Three of the items were originally part of the scale called Material Environment from the Science Laboratory Environment Inventory (Fraser, Giddings, & McRobbie, 1995), but we felt that these items better described the physical space. Two items were used from the Herman Miller Education for Physical Space. Wording for some SLEI items was modified by replacing 'laboratory' with 'classroom' and by eliminating negatively-worded items with reverse scoring (e.g., "I am ashamed of the appearance of this laboratory" became "I like the appearance of this classroom"). Barnette (2000) reported that reverse scoring was *not* effective and recommended using directly-worded stems with bi-directional response options. Taking heed of this recommendation, a few items from other instruments were also slightly modified so that none of the items on the ALES required reverse scoring. Material Environment was also part of the ALES and we used two of its original items along with three Herman Miller items. In total, the ALES has 12 scales with five items per scale making a total of 60 items. Frequency response options are 1 – Almost Never, 2 – Seldom, 3 – Sometimes, 4 – Often, and 5 – Almost Always.

Table 5.2 lists the items in the two scales that specifically address the design of a classroom. It should be noted that there are similarities with Zandvliet's (2014) SPACES. Items in his Spatial Environment scale, and Scale and Esthetics scale were similar to those included in our Physical Space, and items in his Architectural Elements scale were similar to those in our Material Environment. None of our items assessed whether students were comfortable with the temperature in classrooms or the nature/quality of lighting as in SPACES. However, because both of our classrooms were located in the same building and had the same number and type of windows, we did not consider assessing these features.

2.3.2 Videotape Recordings of Student Behaviours

Three camcorders were used in each of the control and experimental classrooms to video-record all lessons throughout the semester. Ten class periods, evenly spaced throughout the semester, were randomly selected and then 10-minute periods near the start and middle of each 80-minute period were identified. The 10-minute samples, as close as possible, showed the same instruction and classroom activities in both environments.

2.3.3 Course Grade and GPA

Final course grades and students' grade point averages (GPAs) were collected by the researchers.

2.4 Qualitative Data Collection

Semi-structured interviews were conducted with five students over the two semesters. An interview was conducted with the person who was the instructor during the fall of 2014 and who was also one of the researchers (Williams). He kept a reflective journal throughout the semester as well. The student interviews were audio-recorded on an iPhone while the instructor interview was undertaken with a camcorder.

2.5 Analysis of Quantitative Data

Survey. The average item means for each of the 12 scales of the ALES were calculated. Scale means for the experimental group (purposefully-designed, active learning classroom) were compared with the control group (traditional classroom).

2.5.1 Videotape Recordings of Student Behaviours

The videotape footage was analysed using a software program called TopScan by Clever Sys Inc., from a bioinformatics company that helps scientists to analyse animal behaviours, typically rodents. The program was previously used in a neuroscience laboratory established by one of the authors, a neurobiologist (Hohmann), to quantify the behaviour of mice during her experimental work (Hohmann, Hodges, Beard, & Aneni, 2013). For many organisms, the physical and social complexity of an environment affects its ability to perform learning and memory tasks (Mohammed et al., 2002; Sale, Hannan, Maffei, & Guzzetta, 2013). We hypothesised that the same procedure would work if applied to our human participants because we were essentially interested in measuring among students similar behaviours to those that had been recorded with mice. Intuitively, it seems logical that a stimulating and enriched environment that demands less sitting in chairs and more physical movement is better for learning. Indeed, cognitive neuroscientists have empirical evidence to show that physical activities such as moving, stretching and walking can enhance the learning process and performance (Jensen, 2000).

After the videotapes were archived, students in both classrooms were given a number by two graduate student 'raters' who were blind to the students' identity. The raters coded five behaviours for all 49 students by using one of five keystrokes on a computer keyboard previously programmed

IMPACT OF A PURPOSEFULLY-DESIGNED ACTIVE LEARNING SPACE 83

TABLE 5.1 Overview of scales (in italics) from four instruments used to create the architecture learning environment survey (ALES)

Instrument	References	Level of usage	No. of scales used	Scales classified according to Moos' scheme			
				Relationship dimensions	Personal development dimensions	System maintenance and change dimensions	
What Is Happening In this Class? (WIHIC)	Fraser, Fisher & McRobbie (1996); Aldridge, Fraser & Huang (1999)	Secondary and Higher Education	All 7	*Student Cohesiveness* *Instructor Support* *Involvement*	*Investigation* *Task Orientation* *Cooperation*	*Equity*
College & University Classroom Environment Inventory (CUCEI)	Fraser & Treagust (1986); Fraser, Treagust & Dennis (1986)	Higher Education	1/7	Personalization Involvement Student Cohesiveness Satisfaction	Task Orientation *Innovation*	Individualization
Constructivist Learning Environment Survey (CLES)	Taylor, Dawson & Fraser (1995); Taylor, Fraser & Fisher (1997)	Secondary and Higher Education	1/5	*Personal Relevance* Uncertainty	Critical Voice Shared Control	Student Negotiation
Science Laboratory Environment Inventory (SLEI)	Fraser, Giddings & McRobbie (1995); Fraser, McRobbie & Giddings (1993)	Upper Secondary and Higher Education	2/5	Student Cohesiveness	*Open-Endedness* Integration	Rule Clarity *Material Environment*

TABLE 5.2 Scales and items from the architecture learning environment survey (ALES) that specifically assess the physical features of a learning space

Scale	Item	Source
Physical Space	I find that the classroom is NOT crowded when I am doing activities.	SLEI[a]
	I like the appearance of this classroom.	SLEI
	This classroom has enough room for both individual and group work.	SLEI
	I am able to see all the students in this class.	Herman Miller[b]
	I have no problem hearing the instructor in this class.	Herman Miller
Material Environment	I find the seating comfortable.	Herman Miller
	I have an adequate amount of surface space to do my work.	Herman Miller
	I am encouraged to move chairs, tables, and other things to help my learning.	Herman Miller
	The equipment in this classroom is in good working order.	SLEI
	The equipment and materials that I need are readily available.	SLEI

a Science Laboratory Environment Inventory (Fraser, Giddings, & McRobbie, 1995).
b Herman Miller Education.

into Clever Sys by Dr Hohmann's student, Lakeisha Lewter (fourth author), who also established the study protocol and trained the graduate student raters in the use of Clever Sys. Interrater reliability was established at 90%. The behaviours were measured for each student as the number of seconds engaged in the behaviour during the 10-minute (600-second) sampling period. Data were entered into an Excel spreadsheet and then into SPSS-11.0 for statistical analysis. The average time in seconds in a 600-second period when each student was involved in each of the following behaviours was calculated:

– *Movement*: Student is out of his/her seat and moving about the classroom space (e.g., going to another group but not interacting with them yet).
– *Student-to-Student Interaction*: Student is engaging in course content-related conversation with another student or showing joint attention on a group task.

- *Student-to-Instructor Interaction*: Student is focusing on or talking with the instructor, or looking at material assigned by the instructor (e.g., reading a handout, watching a video).
- *Interaction with the Physical Environment*: Student is interacting with features in the classroom such as writing on a whiteboard, using a computer or presenting with a projected image in front of the class or small group.
- *Disengagement*: Student is clearly not engaging with the instructor, class materials, or classmates (e.g., gazing out the window, head down and sleeping on desk, texting/emailing on cell phone).

2.5.2 Academic Performance

We believed that students' GPAs would be an accurate predictor of their academic performance in the course. Consequently, average class grades were calculated for both groups, along with the average GPA. Finally, a ratio (class grade/class GPA) was used to reflect the accuracy of the prediction versus reality.

2.6 Analysis of Qualitative Data

Audio recordings of the student and instructor interviews were transcribed. Quotes were extracted from the students' responses. The instructor's responses were summarised and are presented as a narrative in the Results section.

3 Results

Of the 49 students in the study, 22 of the 29 students in the control group completed the survey (76% response rate) compared with 19 of the 20 students in the experimental group (95% response rate).

When looking at the survey results based on Moos' three-dimensional model, the System Maintenance and Change dimension was associated with the largest differences (see Figure 5.2) between the control (traditional) and experimental (enriched, active learning) group. For the four scales in this dimension –Innovation, Material Environment, Equity and Physical Space – only Equity had an average item mean that was higher in the control group, although the difference was only 0.11 and not statistically significant. Therefore, in both groups, during both semesters and with two different instructors, students felt that they were treated equally by their instructor with a frequency of Often to Almost Always. Average item means were higher in the experimental group for Innovation, Material Environment and Physical Space, with differences of 0.38, 0.14 and 0.59, respectively. Interestingly, even though almost all variables were controlled in the two classroom settings, students perceived that their instructor exhibited more innovation in the enriched, active learning classroom. Because the aim of our study was to evaluate the impact of a purposefully-designed classroom, Material Environment and Physical Space were indeed manipulated as described earlier (technology enhancements, additional whiteboards, round tables and chairs on wheels instead of traditional furniture).

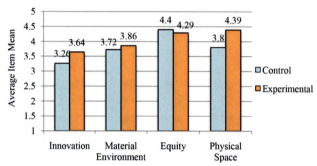

FIGURE 5.2 Average item means for four variables in Moos' system maintenance and change dimension comparing architecture students' perceptions in the control (traditional) group ($n_1 = 22$) and in the experimental (enriched, active learning) group ($n_2 = 19$)

Figure 5.3 summarises the survey results for Moos' Personal Development dimension. Average item means for all scales were higher in the control group. Differences for the scales of Open-Endedness, Investigation, Task Orientation and Cooperation were 0.12, 0.22, 0.14 and 0.08, respectively. All differences were statistically nonsignificant. In particular, Task Orientation had the highest average item mean for both groups (4.56 – Control; 4.42 – Experimental). This indicates that students in both groups felt it was important to complete the instructor's planned activities and to stay focused on the subject matter.

Figure 5.4 indicates that, for Moos' Relationship dimension, average item means were higher for Personal Relevance, Student Cohesiveness and Involvement in the control group. Differences were 0.25, 0.05 and 0.22, respectively, but statistically nonsignificant. For Instructor Support, the average item mean was higher in the experimental group, but by only 0.01 and statistically nonsignificant. The latter finding is important because, each semester, the same instructor taught both the control and experimental classes. Students reported that their instructor helped, befriended, trusted and showed an interest in them with the same frequency

IMPACT OF A PURPOSEFULLY-DESIGNED ACTIVE LEARNING SPACE   87

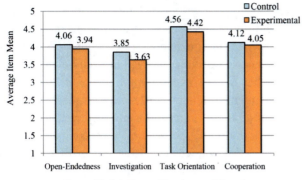

FIGURE 5.3   Average item means of four variables in Moos' personal development dimension comparing architecture students' perceptions in the control (traditional) group ($n_1 = 22$) and in the experimental (enriched, active learning) group ($n_2 = 19$)

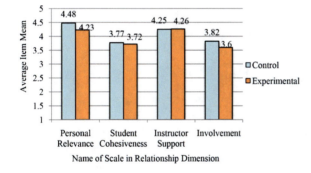

FIGURE 5.4   Average item means of four variables in Moos' relationship dimension comparing architecture students' perceptions in the control (traditional) group ($n_1 = 22$) and in the experimental (enriched, active learning) group ($n_2 = 19$)

in both classroom settings, namely, Often to Almost Always (4.25 – Control; 4.26 – Experimental).

3.1   *Videotaped Recordings of Student Behaviors*

The average time in seconds per 600-second sampling period in the control and experimental groups varied across the five coded behaviours (see Figure 5.5). Student-to-Instructor Interactions were statistically significantly higher ($p<0.01$) in the control group (347 seconds versus 195 seconds). This indicates that, in the traditional classroom with traditional desks, chairs that do not readily move, an obvious 'front of the room', lecturer's podium and large projection screen, students engaged more with the instructor and less with each other. There was also more Movement within the control group (13 seconds versus 8 seconds), but this difference was not statistically significant.

For Student-to-Student Interaction, Interaction with the Physical Environment, and Disengagement, the average time involved in each behaviour was statistically significantly higher for the experimental group ($p<0.01$). Most prominent, with regard to Student-to-Student Interaction, students engaged with each other 81% more or 1.8 times more in the enriched, active learning classroom compared with the traditional classroom (149 seconds – Control; 270 seconds – Experimental). Also noteworthy is the finding that students' Interaction with the Physical Environment was more than double in the enriched, active learning environment (70 seconds – Control; 143 seconds – Experimental). Disengagement was higher in the enriched, active learning classroom.

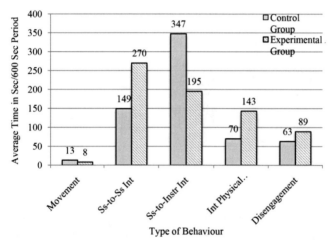

FIGURE 5.5 Results of coding five types of behaviour – movement, student-to-student interaction, student-to-instructor interaction, interaction with the physical environment, and disengagement – that students engaged in during the course, design and human behaviour, spring and fall semesters of 2014 (N = 49)

3.2 *Academic Performance*

Table 5.3 shows that the two groups of students began the course with comparable GPAs (average of 2.77 on a 4-point scale, indicating a C+ average). However, average class grade was statistically significantly higher ($t=2.089$, $p<0.05$) for the experimental group (2.95) compared with the control group (2.33) by the end of the semester. This resulted in the predicted performance for the experimental group being slightly higher than expected (1.04 – class grade/GPA) compared to the control group (0.86).

TABLE 5.3   Comparison of average class grade, average GPA, and ratio between class grade divided by overall GPA for architecture students in the control and experimental groups (N = 45)

Classroom type	Average class grade	Average GPA	Ratio (class grade/GPA)
Control/traditional	2.33	2.70	0.86
Experimental/enriched, active learning	2.95	2.84	1.04

3.3 Student Interviews

Because we aimed to evaluate the impact of the purposefully-designed experimental classroom, most of the interview questions focused on uncovering students' opinions about the physical learning space. Five students from the fall 2014 semester were asked: "How did you feel in the active learning classroom?" Bob (a pseudonym), a White third-year student who waited for five years after high school before starting post-secondary education, stated: "I think that it creates a place where you are comfortable enough to discuss. I think there is kind of a relaxed environment that helps you to feel comfortable to speak up and discuss the topics you are studying". Maureen, a fourth-year international student from Brazil who was self-conscious about her English language skills, said something similar: "I felt comfortable … to be myself here and talk with the people who were at my table. I got used to talking more and expressing myself more". Allan, who had his early education in Dubai but later attended a suburban high school, pointed out that: "It's nice to be able to rely on one another equally rather than have strong kids in the class and the kids that … you know … sit in the back". And finally, Harvey, a shy Vietnamese student, implied that he tended to answer questions more in a small group of classmates because: "In a really formal environment, you don't want to answer the question and you don't want people laughing at the wrong answer. But, when there's a normal conversation, if it's wrong, it's wrong – I can learn from them".

Students were also asked: "What about the space encouraged you to interact?" Bob commented on physical features that were unique to the enriched, active learning classroom (see the mobile whiteboards and round tables in Figure 5.6): "If every group has a whiteboard, it's easy to convey those ideas. Then you can see what everyone else is writing. I think it encourages discussion a little more". Ivan, a third-year African-American student in the control group speculated: "I think that, if you are next to two or three other people, it forces you to talk. And if you're facing each other, I think it forces you to hear somebody else's opinion".

Another question was: "How did the space improve your learning in the course?" Three students mentioned how cooperating with peers helped them to learn. Ivan in the control group said that "you learn more from students than you do from teachers sometimes", while Maureen felt that "you have to interact and, when you have to talk about it and when you have to really make yourself part of something, then you learn". Allan seemed to be a self-regulated learner: "I fit right in and the learning, the creative thinking, and the collaboration started almost immediately. So, I was responsible for my learning".

FIGURE 5.6   Photograph of experimental/active learning classroom showing smaller, mobile whiteboards, monitors near each group, round tables and chairs on casters

3.4   *Instructor Interview*

The following narrative is a summary of the experiences and insights of the instructor from the fall 2014 semester. Because Williams (fifth author) was both the instructor and a researcher, this retrospective narrative cannot be disentangled from both perspectives. However, it is also informed by a reflective journal that he kept throughout the semester.

Williams confirmed that the experimental classroom was indeed better at creating a comfortable environment for both him and the students. He acknowledged that the diverse student body created both opportunities and challenges. It seemed to him that richer discussions occurred in the active learning classroom and multiple views were often expressed. He pointed out that a diverse class is also associated with a range of academic preparedness. Many students balance university with having to work and these students have less time to prepare for class and/or less time to use for completing assignments and projects (relates to ALES scale of Task Orientation). Williams felt that the active learning environment helped the less-prepared students by allowing them to witness how classmates at their table constructed their thoughts while explaining concepts in their own words.

Williams felt it was much easier to facilitate active learning in a classroom specifically designed for it. As Figure 5.7 clearly shows and our 2015 report explains:

> The biases of the traditional classroom became abundantly clear when trying to group students. The rows of computer stations and desks in the traditional classroom made face-to-face communication between students difficult. The instructor could not sit down to join a group seated at a table as a collaborator; rather, he had to roam the space between rows, awkwardly standing and peering down at student groups as an instructor, at best, or judge, at worst. The physicality of the instructor's position and role had a significant effect on student behaviour. Collaborative work in

FIGURE 5.7   Photograph of architecture students and the instructor (third from right) in the experimental/active learning classroom involved in a discussion

the traditional classroom tended to be more quiet and discreet, almost as if the groups did not want the instructor to hear thoughts in progress or questions being sorted through. However, in the active learning classroom, from the moment the instructor joined the group in a seated position around the round table, he was not only able to observe the discussion without change in tone or intensity, but also often able to participate in the discussion and guide it as a fellow thinker. (Determan et al., 2015, p. 23)

4 Discussion

This pilot study aimed to evaluate the impact of an enriched, active learning space that was specifically designed for undergraduate students enrolled in an architecture course called Design and Human Behavior. Results from all four modes of data collection and analyses – survey, videotapes of lessons, grades and interviews – yielded findings that were expected, unexpected and illuminating. Yes, we expected to see a positive impact on learning for those students in the enriched, active learning classroom, but the magnitude of some differences was unexpected. Results were illuminating for three reasons. First, despite not being in the enriched, active learning classroom, students still felt that the instructors treated them equitably and were supportive in both settings to the same degree. Second, there was *more* disengagement in the enriched, active learning classroom, perhaps because the students said that the environment was more comfortable (therefore, more informal). Third, students' academic performance was better or worse than predicted seemingly because of the design of the space. The following paragraphs discuss and interpret the findings in more detail.

4.1 *Architecture Learning Environment Survey*
4.1.1 System Maintenance and Change

As suggested in the previous paragraph, the lack of a significant difference between the two groups for the scale of Equity is seen as a positive outcome (4.40 – Control; 4.29 – Experimental). Whether students are in a student-centred or a teacher-centred learning environment, it is hoped that students would feel that they are being regarded in a consistent and fair manner by an instructor who teaches the same course but in two different classroom settings. This is in contrast to what Walker, Brooks, and Baepler (2011) found with their classroom observation instrument. They found that the instructor modified her behaviour depending on the classroom environment including having more group activities, spending less time at the lectern, and doing more consulting with students in the active learning classroom.

In an enriched, active learning environment, students perceived that their instructors were better able to plan new and unusual activities, engage in innovative teaching techniques and create innovative assignments (3.26 – Control; 3.64 – Experimental). This is despite the fact that the syllabi, class activities/projects, quizzes and homework assignments were the same for both groups. A purposefully-designed active learning classroom could be subconsciously seen as *the* innovation by students, and this might explain why they felt that instructors were engaging in more novel pedagogy when, in fact, pedagogy and class activities were virtually the same in both classrooms.

Perhaps not surprisingly, for Material Environment (3.72 – Control; 3.86 – Experimental) and Physical Space (3.80 versus 4.39), the average item means was higher in the enriched, active learning group. The classroom was intentionally changed from the traditional style in order to promote more effective learning. Looking again at the items in these scales (see Table 5.2), five out of the 10 statements: ("This classroom has enough room for both individual and group work", "I am able to see all the students in this class", "I find the seating comfortable", "I have an adequate amount of surface space to do my work" and "I am encouraged to move chairs, tables, and other things to help my learning") clearly indicate why the average item means are significantly higher in the enriched, active learning environment.

4.1.2 Personal Development

It was not unexpected that the average item means for three Personal Development dimensions – Open-Endedness, Investigation, and Task Orientation – were more or less the same in both groups. However, we were surprised that Cooperation was not higher in the enriched, active learning classroom because of the arrangement of the tables in a circular fashion, mobile whiteboards, and digital monitors near each group. For some unknown reason, it seems that this scale from the ALES was not sensitive enough to cross-validate the findings from the coded student behaviours that were videotaped. Results from the coding unequivocally showed that Student-to-Student Interaction was statistically significantly higher in the enriched, active learning space (149 seconds – Control; 270 seconds – Experimental). Also, during the interviews with students and the instructor, the word 'collaboration' was commonly used.

4.1.3 Relationship Dimensions

Of the four variables in this dimension – Personal Relevance, Student Cohesiveness, Investigation and Instructor Support – the first three had higher average item means in the traditional classroom, but differences were not statistically significant. The difference was only 0.01 for Instructor Support in favour of the experimental group. Similar to Equity in the System Maintenance and Change dimension, this lack of a difference is considered a positive outcome. Instructors can rest assured that, despite the design of the space in which they might find themselves, if other factors such as course content, pedagogy, assignments, projects and homework are consistent, students will still perceive them as helpful, trustworthy and caring.

4.2   Student Behaviours

Videotaping every single lesson in both classrooms over two, 15-week semesters (2 meetings per week; 160 minutes per week) created an enormous amount of footage. Randomly selecting 10 classes per semester, and then sampling 10 minutes within these classes, was a wise decision. We would certainly recommend that other researchers follow this protocol because it yielded more than enough data to code 49 students' behaviours. We are unaware of any other study that has used the Topscan program by Clever Sys to investigate the link between student behaviours in the same course, but in two different spaces, and student outcomes.

Results of the coding clearly show that one environment was teacher-centred and one was student-centred, despite the fact that the pedagogy was kept constant. Students in the traditional classroom interacted with the instructor for an average of 347 seconds per sampling period compared with 195 seconds in the enriched, active learning classroom. In other words, students interacted with their instructor 78% more in the traditional classroom. So what were the students doing in the active learning classrooms if they were not interacting with the instructor? It seems that they were interacting more with each other because Student-to-Student Interaction was 81% higher compared with the traditional classroom – 149 seconds versus 270 seconds. Students were also interacting twice as much with the built environment – 70 seconds versus 143 seconds.

If students are in a comfortable setting, this could lead to more off-task behaviours. Students were Disengaged 41% more in the active learning classroom compared with the traditional classroom. Because comfortable implies informal, students had more opportunities to digitally connect – something to be aware of if instructors find themselves teaching in an active learning classroom. Nevertheless, student performance was higher in this environment, perhaps suggesting that some time off-task is not a detriment in an otherwise engaging setting. Indeed, cognitive neuroscientists have known for a long time that movement actually enhances the learning process (Jensen, 2000). When students move, they increase their circulation and heart rate which increases performance (Tomporowski & Ellis, 1986).

Moving in any classroom is better than being sedentary because a new spatial reference is established and this creates new mental maps that stimulate the brain (Rizzolatti, Fadiga, Fogassi, & Gallese, 1997). Stretching increases the cerebrospinal fluid flow to areas in the brain (Henning, Jacques, Kissel, & Sullivan, 1997) and taking a break from learning (our coded behaviour called Disengagement) is necessary for memory formation (Pelligrini, Huberty, & Jones, 1995). The brain's hippocampus organises and reroutes incoming information (Spitzer, 1997) to the cortex for long-term memory. Because the hippocampus needs time to do this, stuffing it with more and more content yields no new learning. Lastly, movement stimulates the release of noradrenaline and dopamine, chemical neurotransmitters that can improve student motivation. Overall, when we consider the contributions of cognitive science to our understanding of how students learn, we realise that an over fixation on staying 'on task' every minute is unrealistic and probably even harmful to deep learning.

4.3 *Academic Performance*

Studies at the University of Minnesota also focused on students' predicted academic performance, but used the average American College Test (ACT) score to produce their freshmen's ratio (Brooks, 2011; Whiteside, Brooks, & Walker, 2010). Because our students were mostly third- and fourth-year students, they had already taken dozens of courses to generate a college Grade Point Average (GPA). We felt that GPA was a more accurate predictor of their eventual course grade than ACT.

Average course grade was higher in the experimental group (2.95, slightly less than a B) compared with the control group (2.33, closer to a C average than to a B). When students' average course grade was divided by their average GPA, a ratio of 0.86 resulted for the traditional group and 1.04 for students in the enriched, active learning classroom; this was a statistically-significant difference ($p<0.05$). This suggests that students in the experimental group performed as expected but students in the traditional classroom underperformed. These results are in contrast to the University of Minnesota study that used the ACT score in that their researchers found students in the active learning classroom exceeded expectations (Whiteside, Brooks, & Walker, 2010).

4.4 *Interviews*

It is always insightful to hear students' own voices. Interview responses from students in the enriched, active learning classroom supported some, but not all, of the quantitative findings. Overall, closer alignment occurred between the interview responses and the coded videotaped behaviors, than between interview responses and the survey. However, it must be noted that interview questions were not created with the sole purpose of cross-validating *all* scales on the survey. It seems likely that the nature of the interview questions suggested to students in the experimental group that they were part of something unique (i.e., novelty effect) and this could have influenced their responses. Nevertheless, all students conveyed that they had a positive experience that seemed to break down stereotypical barriers between diverse students and allowed them to interact more easily and to learn from each other despite cultural differences.

5   Conclusions and Implications

Results from the ALES showed that four of the 12 scales – Innovation, Instructor Support, Material Environment and Physical Space – had higher average means for students in the active learning environment. The greatest differences were for Material Environment and Physical Space, which we expected because we purposefully designed one classroom to make it an enriched, active learning space. We realise that our sample size was small and that this could have contributed to the unremarkable differences for the other eight scales. Alternatively, *not* finding huge differences between students' perceptions of the two learning environments might not necessarily be negative. For example, we found that students perceived their instructors as equitable and supportive to the same degree when they used active learning pedagogy, irrespective of the type of classroom. Additionally, it must be noted that the ALES was complemented by other data gathering methods. We hope that learning environment researchers will consider using the Topscan program by Clever Sys in their work to investigate correlations between student behaviours that have been reliably quantified and students' perceptions of their learning environment. A better understanding of the strength or weakness of the link between behaviour and perception has significant educational implications.

For decades, researchers across several different fields have known that variables within the learning environment affect how well a student learns (Altman, 1975; Earthman, 2004; Fraser, 2001, 2012; Moos, 1974, 1979; Sommer, 1965, 1969; Walberg, 1991) but, only recently as our study exemplifies, have transdisciplinary teams begun to collaborate on educational projects. With the construction of new school and post-secondary buildings along with the redesign of old, outdated classrooms in existing buildings, it seems that there is finally recognition that we are no longer in the 'assembly line' era of education. Along with the new spaces, pedagogical change is underway. "Active learning is for educators who understand the science behind the learning" (Jensen, 2000, p. 37). The sage on the stage lectures in a teacher-centred environment are being replaced by student-centred environments where active learning during group work is the norm. Rows of desks or tables can stifle creativity, communication, collaboration and critical thinking – traits often identified as essential 21st century skills. To nurture 21st century skills, we must plan and design new and innovative learning spaces, and then show through research-based evidence how, why and in what specific ways these spaces lead to more effective learning.

Research on post-secondary learning environments is still relatively recent (Zandvliet, 2014). Across post-secondary institutions, HBCUs are unique in the US, but they have not been studied as a system, sub-system (e.g., investigating the four HBCUs in the state of Maryland; comparing private versus public HBCUs) or at a single institutional level. Besides the interesting racial make-up at Morgan State, class size is typically small (41% of classes have less than 20 students), suggesting that a learning environment study focusing exclusively on student–teacher relationships (e.g., using the Questionnaire on Teacher Interactions; Wubbels & Levy, 1993) and/or student-to-student interactions could prove interesting and make a distinctive contribution to the field.

Post-secondary classrooms in the US and probably in other countries as well will continue to become more diverse in the future. It is estimated that, by the year 2018, minority students under the age of 18 years will be the majority (Frey, 2012). O'Hare (2011) reports that already there are 10 states in the US that have majority non-White populations of youth. If we want students to be more engaged in active learning and instructors to spend less time lecturing, we must intentionally design classroom spaces to foster more student-to-student interactions. Only through this chain of events will the new generation of post-secondary classroom learning environments create spaces that promote intercultural understanding and empathy in our ever-increasing global communities.

References

Aldridge, J. M., Fraser, B. J., & Huang, I. T.-C. (1999). Investigating classroom environments in Taiwan and Australia with multiple research methods. *Journal of Educational Research, 93*, 48–62.

Altman, I. (1975). *The environment and social behavior: Privacy, personal space, territory, crowding.* Monterey, CA: Brooks/Cole.

Barnette, J. (2000). Effects of stem and Likert response option reversals on survey internal consistency: If you feel the need, there is a better alternative to using those negatively worded stems. *Educational and Psychological Measurement, 60*, 361–370.

Beichner, R., Saul, J., Abbott, D., Morse, J., Deardoff, D., Allain, R., Bonham, S., Dancey, M., & Risley, J. (2007). Student-centered activities for large enrollment undergraduate programs (SCALE-UP) project. In E. Redish & P. Cooney (Eds.), *Research-based reform of university physics* (Reviews in PER Vol. 1). College Park, MD: American Association of Physics Teachers.

Brooks, D. (2011). Space matters: The impact of formal learning environments on student learning. *British Journal of Educational Technology, 42*(5), 719–726.

Brooks, D. (2012). Space and consequences: The impact of different formal learning spaces on instructor and student behavior. *Journal of Learning Spaces, 1*(2), 1–10.

Cleveland, B., & Fisher, K. (2014). The evaluation of physical learning environments: A critical review of the literature. *Learning Environments Research, 17*(1), 1–28.

Determan, J., Akers, M., Williams, I., Hohmann, C., & Martin-Dunlop, C. (2015). Learning space design for the ethnically diverse undergraduate classroom. *Journal for the Society of College and University Planning* (Online). Retrieved from http://www.scup.org/page/resources/books/lsdeduc

Dori, Y., & Belcher, J. (2005). How does technology-enabled active learning affect undergraduate students' understanding of electromagnetism concepts? *The Journal of Learning Sciences, 14*(2), 243–279.

Dori, Y., Belcher, J., Besette, M., Danziger, M., McKinney, A., & Hult, E. (2003). Technology for active learning. *Materials Today, 6*, 44–49.

Earthman, G. (2004). *Prioritization of 31 criteria for school building adequacy*. Baltimore, MD: American Civil Liberties Union Foundation of Maryland.

Fisher, K. (Ed.). (2016). *The translational design of schools: An evidence-based approach to aligning pedagogy and learning environments*. Rotterdam, The Netherlands: Sense Publishers.

Fraser, B. J. (2001). Twenty thousand hours: Editor's introduction. *Learning Environments Research, 4*, 1–5.

Fraser, B. J. (2012). Classroom learning environments: Retrospect, context and prospect. In B. J. Fraser, K. G. Tobin, & C. J. McRobbie (Eds.), *Second international handbook of science education* (pp. 1191–1232). New York, NY: Springer.

Fraser, B. J., Anderson, G. J., & Walberg, H. J. (1982). *Assessment of learning environments: Manual for Learning Environment Inventory (LEI) and My Class Inventory (MCI)* (3rd ed.). Perth: Western Australian Institute of Technology.

Fraser, B. J., Fisher, D. L., & McRobbie, C. J. (1996, April). *Development, validation, and use of personal and class forms of a new classroom environment instrument*. Paper presented at the annual meeting of the American Educational Research Association, New York, NY.

Fraser, B. J., Giddings, G. J., & McRobbie, C. J. (1995). Evolution and validation of a personal form of an instrument for assessing science laboratory classroom environments. *Journal of Research in Science Teaching, 32*, 399–422.

Fraser, B. J., McRobbie, C. J., & Giddings, G. J. (1993). Development and cross-national validation of a laboratory classroom environment instrument for senior high school science. *Science Education, 77*, 1–24.

Fraser, B. J., & Treagust, D. F. (1986). Validity and use of an instrument for assessing classroom psychosocial environment in higher education. *Higher Education, 15*, 37–57.

Fraser, B. J., Treagust, D. F., & Dennis, N. C. (1986). Development of an instrument for assessing classroom psychosocial environment at universities and colleges. *Studies in Higher Education, 11*, 43–54.

Freeman, S., Eddy, S., McDonough, M., Smith, M., Okoroafor, N., Jordt, H., & Wenderoth, M. (2014). Active learning increases student performance in science, engineering, and mathematics. *Proceedings of the National Academy of Sciences, 111*(23), 8410–8415.

Frey, W. (2012). *Census projects new "majority minority" tipping points.* Washington, DC: Brookings Institution.

Gaffney, J., Richards, E., Kustusch, M., Ding, L., & Beichner, R. (2008). Scaling up education reform. *Journal of College Science Teaching, 37*(5), 48–53.

Gislason, N. (2010). Architectural design and the learning environment: A framework for school design research. *Learning Environments Research, 13*, 127–145.

Henning, R., Jacques, P., Kissel, G., & Sullivan, A. (1997). Frequent short breaks from computer work: Effects on productivity and well-being at two field sites. *Ergonomics, 40*(1), 78–91.

Hestenes, D., Wells, M., & Swackhamer, G. (1992). Force concept inventory. *The Physics Teacher, 30*(3), 141–158.

Hohmann, C., Hodges, A., Beard, N., & Aneni, J. (2013). Effects of brief stress exposure during early postnatal development in balb/CByJ mice: I. behavioral characterization. *Developmental Psychobiology, 55*(3), 283–293.

Imms, W., Cleveland, B., & Fisher, K. (Eds.). (2016). *Evaluating learning environments: Snapshots of emerging issues, methods and knowledge.* Rotterdam, The Netherlands: Sense Publishers.

Jensen, E. (2000). Moving with the brain in mind. *Educational Leadership, 58*(3), 34–37.

Mohammed, A., Zhu, S., Darmopil, S., Hjerling-Leffler, J., Ernfors, P., Winblad, B., Diamond, M., Eriksson, P., & Bogdanov, N. (2002). Environmental enrichment and the brain. *Progress in Brain Research, 138*, 109–133.

Moos, R. H. (1974). *The social climate scales: An overview.* Palo Alto, CA: Consulting Psychologists Press.

Moos, R. H. (1979). *Evaluating educational environments.* San Francisco, CA: Jossey-Bass.

Oblinger, D. (2006). Leading the transition from classrooms to learning spaces. *EDUCAUSE Quarterly, 28*(1), 14–18. Retrieved from http://www.educause.edu/research-and-publications/books/learning-spaces

O'Hare, W. (2011). *The changing child population of the United States: Analysis of data from the 2010 census* (KIDS COUNT Working Paper). Baltimore, MD: Annie E. Casey Foundation.

Oluwatayo, A., Aderonmu, P., & Aduwo, E. (2015). Architecture students' perceptions of their learning environment and their academic performance. *Learning Environments Research, 18*, 129–142.

Pellegrini, A., Huberty, P., & Jones, I. (1995). The effects of recess timing on children's playground and classroom behaviors. *American Educational Research Journal, 32*(8), 845–864.

Prince, M. (2004). Does active learning work? A review of the research. *Journal of Engineering Education, 93*(3), 223–231.

Rizzolatti, G., Fadiga, L., Fogassi, L., & Gallese, V. (1997). Enhanced: The space around us. *Science, 277*(5323), 190–191.

Sale, A., Hannan, A., Maffei, L., & Guzzetta, A. (2013). Noninvasive strategies to optimize brain plasticity: From basic research to clinical perspectives. *Neural Plasticity* (Online). Retrieved from http://dx.doi.org/10.1155/2013/863970

Scott-Webber, L., Strickland, A., & Ring Kapitula, L. (2013). Built environments impact behaviors: Results of an active learning post-occupancy evaluation. *Planning for Higher Education Journal, 42*(1), 1–12.

Sommer, R. (1965). Further studies of small group ecology. *Sociometry, 28*(4), 337–348.

Sommer, R. (1969). *Personal space: The behavioral basis of design.* Englewood Cliffs, NJ: Prentice Hall.

Spitzer, M. (1997). *The mind within the net.* Cambridge, MA: MIT Books.

Taylor, P. C., Dawson, V., & Fraser, B. J. (1995, April). *Classroom learning environments under transformation: A constructivist perspective.* Paper presented at annual meeting of American Educational Research Association, San Francisco, CA.

Taylor, P. C., Fraser, B. J., & Fisher, D. L. (1997). Monitoring constructivist classroom learning environments. *International Journal of Educational Research, 27*, 293–302.

Tomporowski, P., & Ellis, N. (1986). Effects of exercise on cognitive processes: A review. *Psychological Bulletin, 99*(3), 338–346.

Walberg, H. (1991). Improving school science in advanced and developing countries. *Review of Educational Research, 61*, 25–69.

Walberg, H. J., & Anderson, G. J. (1968). Classroom climate and individual learning. *Journal of Educational Psychology, 59*, 414–419.

Walker, J., Brooks, D., & Baepler, P. (2011). Pedagogy and space: Empirical research on new learning environments. *EDUCAUSE Quarterly, 34*(4). Retrieved from https://er.educause.edu/search?q=pedagogy+and+space&sortBy=relevance&sortOrder=asc&page=1

Whiteside, A., Brooks, D., & Walker, J. (2010). Making the case for space: Three years of empirical research on learning environments. *EDUCAUSE Quarterly, 33*(3). Retrieved from http://er.educause.edu

Wubbels, T., & Levy, J. (Eds.). (1993). *Do you know what you look like: Interpersonal relationships in education.* London: Falmer Press.

Zandvliet, D. (2014). PLACES and SPACES: Case studies in the evaluation of post-secondary, place-based learning environments. *Studies in Educational Evaluation, 41,* 18–28.

CHAPTER 6

Development and Validation of the Questionnaire Assessing Connections to Science (QuACS)

Georgeos Sirrakos, Jr.
Kutztown University of Pennsylvania, Kutztown, Pennsylvania, USA

Barry J. Fraser
Curtin University, Perth, Australia

1   Introduction

In the United States, the physical sciences are unpopular among Science, Technology, Engineering and Mathematics (STEM) fields, attracting only 2–3% of students (Chen, 2013). Given the problem of recruiting students into STEM degree programs (Beede, Julian, Khan, Lehrman, McKittrick, Langdon, & Doms, 2011), introductory physical science courses at two-year and four-year institutions of higher education seem to be fertile ground for recruitment, because many of these students might not typically consider a STEM degree or career. Unfortunately, introductory physical science courses often require the learning of discrete facts without a focus on assisting students to make meaningful connections to content. Thus, aligning with national and international priorities, it is imperative that educators and researchers seek ways to increase higher education students' interest in STEM and encourage their pursuit of STEM-related degrees and careers (President's Council of Advisors on Science and Technology, 2012; Tobin, 1988).

The inclusion of innovative pedagogical practices such as place-based learning and student narratives into otherwise conventional physical science courses has been found to effectively engage students in the learning of science (Campbell, 2005; Epstein, Easton, Murthy, Davidson, de Bruijn, Hayse, Hens, & Lloyd, 2010; Guertin, 2012; Kraal & Regensburger, 2013). First, these pedagogical practices provide students with opportunities to develop their science process skills. Second, students are given opportunities to engage with scientific artifacts that transcend the traditional classroom. Finally, these practices provide students with the space to make meaningful connections between course content and their everyday lives. Much of the existing literature offers only qualitative evidence to support the effectiveness of place-based learning and scientific storytelling. Therefore, we developed an instrument that could quantitatively measure the impact of these practices, using learning environment and student attitude frameworks. In this chapter, we describe the development and validation of the Questionnaire Assessing Connections to Science (QuACS) to assess the impact of place-based learning and scientific storytelling in terms of students' perceptions of the classroom learning environment and their attitudes towards science.

2   Theoretical Framework

2.1   *Assessing Students' Perceptions of the Learning Environment*

According to Fraser (1986), classroom learning environment is defined as the shared perceptions of the students and the teachers in a particular environment. The development and validation of numerous questionnaires has allowed the field of learning environments research to flourish (Fraser, 2012). Beginning with the Learning Environment Inventory (LEI) in the late 1960s, these questionnaires have provided researchers with the ability to gather data that are more authentic by evaluating the learning environment through the eyes of those who are directly experiencing it (Murray, 1938). To develop the Questionnaire Assessing Connections to Science (QuACS), we borrowed and adapted a combination of learning environment scales from the Constructivist Learning Environment Survey (CLES) and the College and University Classroom Environment Inventory (CUCEI). The CLES and CUCEI not only offer quick and effective ways of assessing students' perceptions of the learning environment, but also both have a strong factor structure and proven reliability in a variety of classroom settings. A brief overview of each questionnaire's development and use in research follows.

Taylor and Fraser (1991) developed the CLES as a means of assessing "the degree to which a particular classroom's environment is consistent with a constructivist epistemology" (Fraser, 2007, p. 107). The CLES contains 30 items spread across five scales (Personal Relevance, Uncertainty, Critical Voice, Shared Control and Student Negotiation), with each item scored using the frequency response alternatives of Almost Never, Seldom, Sometimes, Often and Very Often (Fraser, 2007). The scales were developed with the assumption that learning is a complex cognitive process in which students construct knowledge by connecting new and existing ideas to the world around them. Since its development, researchers have used the CLES across the globe to evaluate the effectiveness of innovative curricula (Harwell, Gunter, Montgomery, Shelton, & West, 2001) and teacher development programs (Beck, Czerniak, &

Lumpe, 2000; Cannon, 1995; Ebrahimi, 2015; Nix, Fraser, & Ledbetter, 2005), as well as for investigating students' perceptions of constructivist learning environments in science (Aldridge, Fraser, Taylor, & Chen, 2000; Dryden & Fraser, 1998; Fraser & Lee, 2015; Goh & Fraser, 2016; Johnson & McClure, 2004; Kim, Fisher, & Fraser, 1999; Oh & Yager, 2004; Peer & Fraser, 2015; Peiro & Fraser, 2009; Zeidan, 2015) mathematics (Aldridge, Fraser, & Sebela, 2004; Ogbuehi & Fraser, 2007; Spinner & Fraser, 2005), humanities (Kwan & Wong, 2014), English (Lim, in press; Wilks, 2000), and in classrooms with an emphasis on the use of technology to deliver curriculum (Chuang & Tsai, 2005; Luan, Bakar, Mee, & Ayub, 2010). Many of these studies also supported the instrument's strong factor structure and validity for use across a variety of contexts.

Fraser and Treagust (1986) developed the CUCEI to investigate the learning environments of small higher-education classrooms. Because of similarities between small seminar-type classrooms in tertiary settings and secondary-school classrooms, many of the seven scales included in the CUCEI (Personalization, Involvement, Student Cohesiveness, Satisfaction, Task Orientation, Innovation and Individualization) mirror scales from pre-existing questionnaires that contain scales that are already considered to be relevant as predictors of student outcomes within the secondary classroom. The preliminary version of the CUCEI was field tested with a sample of undergraduate and graduate students at a higher-education institution in Perth, Western Australia. Scale internal consistency and discriminant validity analyses led to a refined version of the CUCEI with 49 items equally distributed among the seven scales. Each item is scored on a four-point scale with response options of Strongly Agree, Agree, Disagree and Strongly Disagree. The refined CUCEI was cross-validated using data collected from students in undergraduate and graduate courses in a variety of disciplines, including education, biology, mathematics, communications and psychology, in higher-education institutions in Western Australia and Illinois, United States (Fraser & Treagust, 1986).

The CUCEI has been used extensively in a variety of research contexts pertaining to higher education. In some studies, the CUCEI (or a modified version of it) was further validated with a different sample. For example, Nair and Fisher (2001) validated a new form of the CUCEI and subsequently used the instrument to investigate the transition of senior secondary-school students to higher-education institutions. Nair and Fisher found that students perceived their tertiary learning environment more negatively than their previous secondary learning environment. In 2014, Dorman (2014) collected data from 495 students from an Australian public university and further confirmed the CUCEI's validity as reported in previous studies. In addition, Dorman revealed that several CUCEI scales served as significant predictors of students' experiences at university.

Thus, Dorman asserted that a focus on the improvement of specific areas of the learning environment covered by CUCEI scales could lead to positive changes in the ways in which students experience their university learning environment. More recently, Hasan and Fraser (2015) used a modified version of the CUCEI to investigate the learning environment in college-level mathematics classes in the United Arab Emirates. Specifically, the researchers studied how the integration of personally-relevant and activity-based teaching strategies impacted adult learners who had previously experienced failure in mathematics. The CUCEI has also been used in several other higher-education studies, including a comparison of the effectiveness of blended and flipped course formats in undergraduate courses (Clark, Kaw, & Besterfield-Sacre, 2016; Strayer, 2012) and an investigation into the relationship between academic dishonesty and college classroom environment (Pulvers & Diekhoff, 1999).

2.2 Measuring Students' Science-Related Attitudes

Our ability to measure students' attitudes towards science has been enhanced by the development and validation of a variety of attitude-oriented instruments. Klopfer (1971) describes attitudes towards science as learning "to value science for its contributions to man's intellectual growth and to society" (p. 443). To develop the attitudes component of the Questionnaire Assessing Connections to Science (QuACS), we borrowed and modified scales from various instruments including the Test of Science-Related Attitudes (TOSRA) (Fraser, 1981a) as well as more-contemporary instruments such as the Students' Attitudes Towards Science (SATS) (Aydeniz & Kotowski, 2014) and the My Attitudes Toward Science (MATS) (Hillman, Zeeman, Tilburg, & List, 2016).

The TOSRA was developed by Fraser (1981a) to assess science-related attitudes among secondary-school students. The instrument contains 70 items divided into seven distinct scales: Social Implications of Science, Normality of Scientists, Attitude to Scientific Inquiry, Adoption of Scientific Attitudes, Enjoyment of Science Lessons, Leisure Interest in Science and Career Interest in Science. Each item is scored 1, 2, 3, 4, and 5, respectively, for the responses of Strongly Disagree, Disagree, Neutral, Agree and Strongly Agree. The TOSRA has been cross-validated with samples of secondary science classes in Australia and the United States, providing additional support for the validity for its use with Australian students, and supporting its cross-cultural validity for use with students in the United States (Fraser & Butts, 1982; Lucas & Tulip, 1980; Schibeci & McGaw, 1981).

The TOSRA (or modified forms of it) has been used in many studies to investigate associations between students' perceptions of the classroom learning environment and students' attitudes (Aldridge & Fraser, 2008; Fraser, Aldridge, & Adolphe, 2010; Sirrakos & Fraser, 2017; Wolf & Fraser, 2008; Wong &

Fraser, 1996). Using a similar approach, Bui and Alfaro (2011) used the TOSRA to examine relationships between anxiety in statistics courses and students' attitudes towards science. In another study, Peer and Fraser (2015) used the TOSRA to explore differences in attitudes related to sex, grade level and stream (gifted education versus high ability) in several middle schools in Singapore. Researchers have also developed modified versions of the TOSRA to explicitly measure students' attitudes in other academic disciplines, including the Test of Geography-Related Attitudes (TOGRA) (Walker, 2006), Test of Spanish-Related Attitudes (TOSRA – L1) (Adamski, Fraser, & Peiro, 2013) and Test of Mathematics-Related Attitudes (TOMRA) (Spinner & Fraser, 2005).

The SATS (Aydeniz & Kotowski, 2014) was developed to address perceived issues in contemporary ways of measuring students' attitudes towards science. Expanding upon existing attitude instruments, the SATS was validated with a sample of 205 students from five schools in the southeastern United States. Data analyses supported the factor structure of a version of the SATS with 28 items across six scales: Attitude Toward Learning Science, Motivations Towards Learning Science, Utility of Science, Self-Efficacy in Science Learning, Normative Beliefs about Science Learning and Intentions to Pursue Science-Related Activities. The MATS is a more-recent instrument that incorporates the multidimensional nature of students' attitudes towards science (Hillman, Zeeman, Tilburg, & List, 2016). After initial content validity checks, the MATS was administered to 549 students in 24 classrooms in the northeast United States. Reliability analyses yielded a final instrument with 40 items in four scales: Attitude towards School Science, Desire to Become a Scientist, Perception of Scientists and Value of Science to Society. Because of the relative newness of each instrument, we are unable to report additional research studies that have made use of these instruments.

2.3   *Evaluating Educational Innovations*

Research that has involved the use of learning environment instruments can generally be categorised into one or more of 12 primary areas of study (Fraser, 2012): associations between outcomes and environment; evaluation of educational innovations; differences between students' and teachers' perceptions of the same classrooms; whether students achieve better in their preferred environment; teachers' use of learning environment perceptions in guiding improvements in classrooms; combining quantitative and qualitative methods; links between different educational environments; cross-national studies; the transition from primary to high school; incorporating educational environment ideas into school psychology (Burden & Fraser, 1993), teacher education, and teacher assessment. The existence of preferred forms of learning environment questionnaires (Byrne, Hattie, & Fraser, 1986) and of convenient short forms (Fraser & Fisher, 1983) has facilitated the implementation of learning environment ideas by practitioners wishing to improve their classroom climates (Fraser, 1981b).

While the Questionnaire Assessing Connections to Science (QuACS) can be used to achieve the aforementioned research objectives, its development fills a gap in the literature by providing opportunities for researchers to further evaluate educational innovations that involve place-based learning, scientific storytelling or narratives. Specifically, we developed the QuACS to assess the impact of integrating place-based learning and scientific storytelling into introductory-level physical science courses at colleges and universities.

Educators employ a repertoire of specific pedagogical strategies and techniques to develop students' science concepts (Treagust, Duit, & Fraser, 1996). Some of these strategies and techniques might not have been previously practised or considered novel. Researchers and educators often refer to these emerging practices as 'educational innovations'. Because the impact of an educational innovation might not be immediately known, it might not be considered worthy of employing on a large scale. However, fortunately, many researchers have evaluated educational innovations by investigating their effects on students' perceptions of the learning environment, their attitudes and/or other criteria of effectiveness.

For example, when Maor and Fraser (1996) used a classroom environment instrument to evaluate the use of a computerised database by exploring changes in students' perceptions of their learning environment, students perceived their classes as becoming more inquiry-oriented during the use of the computerised database. In California, Martin-Dunlop and Fraser (2008) used a combination of scales from two learning environment instruments to evaluate the effectiveness of an innovative science course offered at a large urban university for improving prospective elementary teachers' perceptions of laboratory learning environments and attitudes towards science. Statistically significant differences were found between students' perceptions of the innovative course and their previous courses. Sirrakos and Fraser (2017) conducted a cross-national study to investigate the impact of reality pedagogy on students' perceptions of the learning environment and their attitudes toward science. Reality pedagogy is an approach to teaching that involves the enactment of strategic practices meant to provide teachers with opportunities to immerse themselves in the lived realities of their students. The study revealed that reality pedagogy positively impacted the learning environment perceptions and attitudes towards science of both groups of students.

In addition to the studies described above, many past evaluations of educational innovations have primarily focused on exploring the effect of implementing information technology on the learning environment (e.g. Teh & Fraser, 1995). Fraser (1998, 2002, 2007) notes that most evaluations of technology innovations in the classroom have resulted in changes in how students perceive their classroom environments in terms of dimensions such as involvement, teacher support, task orientation and equity.

2.4   Place-based Learning and Scientific Narratives

One of the overarching problems associated with today's science classrooms is students' inability to make connections with course content (Bonnett, 2004). This lack of connection is often the cause of students' low performance, interest and persistence in the sciences but, according to Sobel (2004), this can be mitigated through place-based learning. In the literature, place-based learning is often used to refer to opportunities for students to engage in some form of outdoor or environmental education. When developing the Questionnaire Assessing Connections to Science (QuACS), we defined place-based learning more broadly as a pedagogical approach that encourages students to engage with their physical and cultural environments by using those as sites of exploration and sense-making (Semken & Freeman, 2008). For example, for a more-robust understanding of the interconnectedness between local and global issues, a visit to a museum, a walk through a university campus, an interview with a community leader or the collection of physical or symbolic artifacts are all ways for students to engage in place-based learning. Epstein et al. (2010) and Guertin (2013) have extensively used place-based learning in undergraduate physical science courses. According to Guertin (2013), place-based learning can fulfill an identified need with and for a community partner and aid students in making connections with classroom work. For example, in a physical science course, students were tasked with developing an awareness campaign to focus on global water issues. These students created a series of podcasts on local and international topics ranging from water conflicts and pollutants to interviews with leaders of non-profit water organisations.

Guertin's approach of having students create narrative podcasts as a mode of scientific communication is not exclusive to place-based learning. However, the approach follows a growing trend towards incorporating multimodal representations of science content (Dhingra, 2008; Kraal & Regensburger, 2013; O'Neill & Calabrese-Barton, 2005). Often, these new media serve as scientific stories, or narratives, and research suggests that narratives are easier to comprehend than traditional logical-scientific forms of communication.

Further, scientific narratives are capable of cultivating students' sense of ownership over the content learned, resulting in increased engagement with the content (Dahlstrom, 2014). Scientific storytelling can be accomplished through the production and distribution of video and/or audio files. Some higher-education physical-science faculty have developed and integrated such assignments into already-existing coursework (Epstein et al., 2010; Guertin, 2012, 2013; Kraal & Regensburger, 2013). Examples of such assignments include describing the results of research, explaining a scientific process or offering specific reflections on course content. According to Malan (2007), these types of assignments offer the "potential not necessarily to educate better but to educate further" (p. 390). However, as previously mentioned, the evaluation of place-based learning and scientific storytelling, particularly in introductory-level science courses, has not been very robust, prompting the development of a new evaluation instrument.

3 Research Methods and Data Sources

3.1 *Developing the Questionnaire Assessing Connections to Science (QuACS)*

In order to determine which scales to include in the QuACS, we asked physical science faculty at several colleges and universities across the United States to think about ways in which students typically connect to science. This iterative process lasted approximately four months while input and feedback was continuously collected. Most of the faculty responses centred on connecting the content to students' lives, demonstrating how students might use science in the future, and engaging students in scientific discussions that require critical thinking. Using this feedback, we evaluated a variety of published instruments and used our findings to develop a preliminary version of the QuACS consisting of seven scales: Personal Relevance, Innovation, Future Intentions to Study Science, Science Self-Efficacy, Communicating Scientifically, Scientific Storytelling and Place-based Learning. We adapted four scales from existing questionnaires and developed three new scales (Communicating Scientifically, Scientific Storytelling and Place-based Learning) using the feedback from science faculty. We developed the latter three scales to assess the extent to which the integration of personal and contextual scientific narratives, along with place-based learning opportunities, would be helpful in connecting students to science. While a review of the literature did not uncover existing learning environment and student attitude questionnaires that could be used to explore educational innovations such as place-based learning (using our broad definition) and scientific narratives, several robust and well-validated instruments already existed to assess the scales of Personal Relevance, Innovation, Future Intentions to Study Science and Science Self-Efficacy. For this reason, we elected to adapt existing scales and items and add them to the three newly-developed scales rather than create an entirely new instrument from scratch.

The preliminary questionnaire consisted of seven scales each with seven items for a total of 49 items. Table 6.1 provides the scale source, a scale description and a sample item for each scale. All items were worded using positive language to improve the overall validity and reliability of the questionnaire (Schriesheim & Eisenbach, 1991). Each item employed a Likert response format and was scored 1, 2, 3, 4 and 5, respectively, for the alternatives of Strongly Disagree, Disagree, Neutral, Agree and Strongly Agree.

3.2 Field-testing the Questionnaire Assessing Connections to Science (QuACS)

While the five questionnaires (CLES, CUCEI, TOSRA, SATS and MATS) from which items were adapted had been previously validated, combining and adapting selected scales and items created a 'new' questionnaire whose validity and reliability might not be consistent with previous research findings. Further, the three new scales which we developed also required validation. Therefore, to establish the QuACS' validity, the preliminary version underwent face validity testing involving two graduate students, two laypersons, two faculty members in science education and two faculty members in the physical sciences. After face validity was established, the instrument was administered to the main sample for further validation.

The instrument was field-tested during March/April 2016 using a sample of 495 undergraduate students who were enrolled in an introductory-level physical science course at an institution of higher education. This type of course is intended for students who do not anticipate pursuing a degree in any of the pure sciences (i.e. biology, chemistry, geology, etc.). The 495 students were sampled from nine classrooms across five institutions which varied in type, student enrollment and geographic area. Of the five institutions, three were public and two were private. The differences in total student enrollment were stark, with one institution enrolling approximately 2,000 students, two institutions enrolling approximately 10,000 students and the other two institutions each enrolling more than 30,000 students. In terms of geography, one of the institutions is located in a rural area, three are in a metropolitan area and one is in an urban area.

TABLE 6.1 Preliminary structure of the questionnaire assessing connections to science (QuACS)

Scale	Source	Description	Sample item	Number of items
Personal relevance	CLES (Taylor & Fraser, 1991)	The extent to which school science connects with students' out-of-school experiences	This course provides me with a better understanding of the world outside school.	7
Innovation	CUCEI (Fraser & Treagust, 1986)	The extent to which the instructor utilises a variety of new activities, teaching techniques and assignments	New and different ways of teaching are used in this class.	7
Future intentions to study science	TOSRA (Fraser, 1981a) MATS (Hillman, Zeeman, Tilburg, & List, 2016).	The extent to which students indicate their intentions to study science in the future or pursue a science-related career	I intend to study science in the future.	7
Science self-efficacy	SATS (Aydeniz & Kotowski, 2014)	The extent to which students believe that they can be successful in science	I am confident I can do well in this science course.	7
Communicating scientifically	Not applicable (Newly developed by researchers)	The extent to which students believe they can successfully communicate scientific information to others	I am able to communicate scientific information verbally and in writing.	7

TABLE 6.1 Preliminary structure of the questionnaire assessing connections to science (QuACS) (cont.)

Scale	Source	Description	Sample item	Number of items
Scientific storytelling	Not applicable (newly developed by researchers)	The extent to which students believe that scientific storytelling assists them in making connections to science	Combining scientific information from several sources into a story is an interesting way to learn science.	7
Place-based learning	Not applicable (newly developed by researchers)	The extent to which students believe that the local community is a good source of science learning	The local community is a useful resource for learning science.	7

4 Data Analyses and Findings

In order to check the structure of the instrument's 49 items in seven a priori scales, we performed several principal axis factor analyses with oblimin rotation and Kaiser normalization. The criteria for the retention of any item were that it must have a factor loading of at least 0.50 with its own scale and less than 0.50 with other scales. Analyses were performed for the total sample of 495 undergraduate university students.

The optimal factor solution emerged when the two learning environment scales were analysed separately from the five attitude scales. Table 6.2 shows that, for the two 7-item learning environment scales of Personal Relevance and Innovation, every item had a factor loading of at least 0.50 with its own scale and less than 0.50 with the other scale. Therefore, all items were retained. The bottom of Table 6.2 shows that the proportion of variance accounted for was

TABLE 6.2 Factor analysis results for learning environment scales

Item	Factor loadings[a]	
	Personal relevance	Innovation
PR 1	0.57	
PR 8	0.74	
PR 15	0.68	
PR 22	0.58	
PR 29	0.68	
PR 36	0.77	
PR 43	0.73	
IN 2		0.73
IN 9		0.79
IN 16		0.76
IN 23		0.71
IN 30		0.87
IN 37		0.68
IN 44		0.83
% Variance	15.09	49.16
Eigenvalue	2.11	6.88
Alpha Reliability	0.88	0.93

a Factor loadings smaller than 0.50 omitted.

49.16% for Innovation and 15.09% for Personal Relevance (total of 64.25%) and eigenvalues for the two scales were 6.88 and 2.11, respectively.

For the five 7-item attitude scales, Table 6.3 shows that the optimal factor structure emerged for a refined version in which (1) all of the 14 items in the two originally-separate Self-Efficacy scales (Science Self-Efficacy and Communicating Scientifically) came together to form a single Science Self-Efficacy scale and (2) two items from Place-Based Learning (PB14 and PB35) were removed because their factor loading with their own scale was less than 0.50. The bottom of Table 6.3 shows that, for the four refined attitude scales, the proportion of variance ranged from 3.74% to 45.57% (total of 69.53%) and eigenvalues ranged from 1.24 to 15.04.

TABLE 6.3 Factor analysis results for attitude scales

Item	Factor loadings[a]			
	Future intentions to study science	Self-efficacy	Scientific storytelling	Place-based learning
FI 3	0.80			
FI 10	0.60			
FI 17	0.84			
FI 24	0.68			
FI 31	0.82			
FI 38	0.83			
FI 45	0.82			
SE 4		0.70		
SE 11		0.73		
SE 18		0.78		
SE 25		0.67		
SE 32		0.78		
SE 39		0.76		
SE 46		0.72		
SE 5		0.64		
SE 12		0.75		
SE 19		0.77		
SE 26		0.75		
SE 33		0.78		
SE 40		0.76		

TABLE 6.3   Factor analysis results for attitude scales (*cont.*)

Item	Factor loadings[a]			
	Future intentions to study science	Self-efficacy	Scientific storytelling	Place-based learning
SE 47		0.75		
SS 6			0.61	
SS 13			0.68	
SS 20			0.58	
SS 27			0.69	
SS 34			0.79	
SS 41			0.64	
SS 48			0.61	
PB 7				0.54
PB 21				0.66
PB 28				0.69
PB 42				0.59
PB 49				0.70
% Variance	11.67	45.57	8.55	3.74
Eigenvalue	3.85	15.04	2.82	1.24
Alpha Reliability	0.94	0.95	0.91	0.89

a   Factor loadings smaller than 0.50 omitted.

We checked the internal consistency of each learning environment and attitude scale by calculating Cronbach's alpha coefficient to ensure that each of the items making up the same scale in the QuACS reflected a common construct. The bottom of Tables 6.2 and 6.3 shows that the alpha reliability was 0.88 and 0.93 for the two learning environment scales and ranged from 0.89 to 0.95 for the four attitude scales. These values indicate high reliability.

Our findings regarding the validity and reliability of the four adapted scales are consistent with past research studies that utilised scales from the CLES, CUCEI, TOSRA, SATS and MATS. Based on our findings, we modified the preliminary version of the QuACS to form the refined version consisting of 47 items across six scales. Table 6.4 presents the scale and item structure for a refined version of the QuACS, while the final version of the QuACS along with scale and item allocations can be found in the Appendix.

TABLE 6.4   Final structure of the questionnaire assessing connections to science

Scale	Description	Sample item	Number of items
Personal Relevance	The extent to which school science connects with students' out-of-school experiences	This course provides me with a better understanding of the world outside school.	7
Innovation	The extent to which the instructor utilises a variety of new activities, teaching techniques and assignments.	New and different ways of teaching are used in this class.	7
Future Intentions to Study Science	The extent to which students indicate their intentions to study science in the future or pursue a science-related career	I intend to study science in the future.	7
Science Self-Efficacy	The extent to which students believe that they can be successful in science and scientific communication	I am confident I can do well in this science course.	14
Scientific Storytelling	The extent to which students believe that scientific storytelling assists them in making connections to science	Combining scientific information from several sources into a story is an interesting way to learn science.	7
Place-based Learning	The extent to which students believe that the local community is a good source of science learning	The local community is a useful resource for learning science.	5

5 Significance and Implications

First, and most importantly, our work described in this chapter fills a gap in learning environment and student attitude research through the development of the Questionnaire Assessing Connections to Science (QuACS). This questionnaire is uniquely designed to assess changes in learning environment perceptions and students' attitudes towards science that occur during place-based learning and scientific storytelling activities in introductory-level science courses at colleges and universities. Further, field-testing of the QuACS with a sample of

495 undergraduate students in introductory level science courses resulted in a refined six-scale, 47-item version that was shown to have sound factorial validity and internal consistency reliability. Finally, a 2013 study by the National Survey of Student Engagement reported that today's college students acquire and process information very differently from the previous generation of college students. This shift has prompted researchers to explore the effectiveness of educational innovations in terms of students' engagement, attitudes and perceptions of the learning environment (Aldridge & Fraser, 2008; Zandvliet & Fraser, 2005). However, Fraser (2007, p. 112) asserts that: "Despite the potential value of evaluating educational innovations and new curricula in terms of their impact on transforming the classroom learning environment, only a relatively small number of such studies have been carried out around the world". Thus, with the QuACS' development, researchers now have an additional tool to use for in-depth research involving the evaluation of educational innovations, particularly those aimed at improving the teaching and learning of science at higher-education institutions.

Appendix
Questionnaire for Assessing Connections to Science (QuACS)

Directions
- This questionnaire contains a number of statements regarding your perceptions of the science learning environment and your attitudes toward science.
- The purpose of this questionnaire is to find out your opinions about your science learning environment and your attitudes toward science.
- For each statement, you will be asked to indicate how much you agree or disagree with that statement. There are no "correct" or "incorrect" answers.
- Read each statement and indicate the extent of your agreement by circling the appropriate number between 1 and 5, where the numbers mean:
  5 – Strongly agree
  4 – Agree
  3 – Neutral (no strong opinion)
  2 – Disagree
  1 – Strongly disagree
- Please circle only ONE number per statement. If you change your mind about your answer, cross it out or erase it and circle another answer.
- Although some statements in this questionnaire are fairly similar to other statements, you are asked to indicate your opinion for all statements.

	Statement	SA	A	N	D	SD
1.	This course provides me with a better understanding of the world outside school.	5	4	3	2	1
2.	New and different ways of teaching are used in this class.	5	4	3	2	1
3.	I intend to study science in the future.	5	4	3	2	1
4.	I am confident I can do well in this science course.	5	4	3	2	1
5.	I am able to communicate scientific information verbally and in writing.	5	4	3	2	1
6.	Combining scientific information from several sources into a story is an interesting way to learn science.	5	4	3	2	1
7.	The local community is a useful resource for learning science.	5	4	3	2	1
8.	The things I learn in this course are relevant to my out-of-school life.	5	4	3	2	1
9.	The instructor creates innovative assignments for students.	5	4	3	2	1
10.	I intend to enroll in another science course before I graduate.	5	4	3	2	1
11.	I am capable of learning difficult science concepts.	5	4	3	2	1
12.	I feel confident participating in a scientific discussion.	5	4	3	2	1
13.	Creating a scientific story is an effective way to learn science.	5	4	3	2	1
14.	What I learn in this course helps me better understand how science impacts my life.	5	4	3	2	1
15.	Teaching approaches in this class are characterized by innovation.	5	4	3	2	1
16.	I will seek opportunities to study science in the future.	5	4	3	2	1
17.	I can earn a good grade in this science course.	5	4	3	2	1
18.	I feel confident talking about science.	5	4	3	2	1
19.	The inclusion of personal stories makes science content interesting.	5	4	3	2	1
20.	Exploring science in the local community helps me better understand science.	5	4	3	2	1
21.	My new learning starts with problems about the world outside school.	5	4	3	2	1
22.	The instructor uses a variety of instructional resources and materials.	5	4	3	2	1
23.	A career in a science-related field would be interesting.	5	4	3	2	1
24.	If I try hard, I can understand difficult science concepts.	5	4	3	2	1

	Statement	SA	A	N	D	SD
25.	I am able to explain science concepts to my classmates.	5	4	3	2	1
26.	Scientific stories are helpful in making personal connections to science.	5	4	3	2	1
27.	Using the local community as a learning tool is an appropriate way to learn science.	5	4	3	2	1
28.	The topics we cover in this course have personal meaning to me.	5	4	3	2	1
29.	This class uses innovative activities and assignments.	5	4	3	2	1
30.	I intend to continue learning science in the future.	5	4	3	2	1
31.	I am confident in my ability to learn science.	5	4	3	2	1
32.	I feel confident in communicating what I learn in science.	5	4	3	2	1
33.	Scientific storytelling is a good way to learn science.	5	4	3	2	1
34.	Science is relevant to my out-of-school life.	5	4	3	2	1
35.	The activities/assignments in this course are different from those in previous/other courses.	5	4	3	2	1
36.	I would like to work in a science-related field when I graduate.	5	4	3	2	1
37.	I believe that I can be successful in this science course.	5	4	3	2	1
38.	I am able to communicate scientific information in several ways.	5	4	3	2	1
39.	Learning through people's personal stories helps me make connections to science.	5	4	3	2	1
40.	Working alongside community members increases my understanding of local scientific issues.	5	4	3	2	1
41.	This course makes me curious about things I encounter outside school.	5	4	3	2	1
42.	The instructor thinks of unique class activities and assignments.	5	4	3	2	1
43.	I look forward to enrolling in more science classes in the future.	5	4	3	2	1
44.	I am able to learn new science concepts.	5	4	3	2	1
45.	I feel confident explaining something learned in this class to another person.	5	4	3	2	1
46.	Scientific stories are effective for explaining science content to a chosen audience.	5	4	3	2	1
47.	Using community resources makes learning science exciting.	5	4	3	2	1

Scale and Item Allocation

Scale name	QuACS item numbers
Learning environment scales	
Personal relevance	1, 8, 14, 21, 28, 34, 41
Innovation	2, 9, 15, 22, 29, 35, 42
Attitude scales	
Future intentions to study science	3, 10, 16, 23, 30, 36, 43
Science self-efficacy	4, 5, 11, 12, 17, 18, 24, 25, 31, 32, 37, 38, 44, 45
Scientific storytelling	6, 13, 19, 26, 33, 39, 46
Place-based learning	7, 20, 27, 40, 47

References

Adamski, A., Fraser, B. J., & Peiro, M. M. (2013). Parental involvement in schooling, classroom environment and student outcomes. *Learning Environment Research, 16*, 315–328.

Aldridge, J. M., & Fraser, B. J. (2008). *Outcomes-focused learning environments: Determinants and effects* (Advances in Learning Environments Research Series). Rotterdam, The Netherlands: Sense Publishers.

Aldridge, J. M., Fraser, B. J., & Sebela, M. P. (2004). Using teacher action research to promote constructivist learning environments in South Africa. *South African Journal of Education, 24*, 245–253.

Aldridge, J. M., Fraser, B. J., Taylor, P. C., & Chen, C. C. (2000). Constructivist learning environments in a cross-national study in Taiwan and Australia. *International Journal of Science Education, 22*, 37–55.

Aydeniz, M., & Kotowski, M. R. (2014). Conceptual and methodological issues in the measurement of attitudes towards science. *Electronic Journal of Science Education, 18*, 1–24.

Beck, J., Czerniak, C. M., & Lumpe, A. T. (2000). An exploratory study of teachers' beliefs regarding the implementation of constructivism in their classroom. *Journal of Science Teacher Education, 11*, 323–343.

Beede, D., Julian, T., Khan, B., Lehrman, R., McKittrick, G., Langdon, D., & Doms, M. (2011). *Education supports racial and ethnic equality in STEM*. Retrieved from http://www.esa.doc.gov/sites/default/files/education_supports_racial_and_ethnic_equality_in_stem.pdf

Bonnett, M. (2004). Lost in space? Education and the concept of nature. *Studies in Philosophy and Education, 23*, 117–130.

Bui, N. H., & Alfaro, M. A. (2011). Statistics anxiety and science attitudes: Age, gender, and ethnicity factors. *College Student Journal, 45*, 573–585.

Burden, R. L., & Fraser, B. J. (1993). Use of classroom environment assessments in school psychology: A British perspective. *Psychology in the Schools, 30*(3), 232–240.

Byrne, D. B., Hattie, J. A., & Fraser, B. J. (1986). Student perceptions of preferred classroom learning environment. *Journal of Educational Research, 80*(1), 10–18.

Campbell, G. (2005). There is something in the air: Podcasting in education. *Educause Review, 40*(6), 32–46.

Cannon, J. R. (1995). Further validation of the constructivist learning environment survey: Its use in the elementary science methods course. *Journal of Elementary Science Education, 7*, 47–62.

Chen, X. (2013). *STEM attrition: College students' paths into and out of STEM fields* (NCES 2014-001). Washington, DC: National Center for Education Statistics, Institute of Education Sciences, U.S. Department of Education. Retrieved April, 2016, from http://nces.ed.gov/pubs2014/2014001rev.pdf

Chuang, S.-C., & Tsai, C.-C. (2005). Preferences toward the constructivist Internet-based learning environments among high school students in Taiwan. *Computers in Human Behavior, 21*, 255–272.

Clark, R. M., Kaw, A., & Besterfield-Sacre, M. (2016). Comparing the effectiveness of blended, semi-flipped, and flipped formats in an engineering numerical methods course. *Advances in Engineering Education, 5*, 1–38.

Dahlstrom, M. F. (2014). Using narratives to communicate science with nonexpert audiences. *Proceedings of the National Academy of Sciences, 111*, 13614–13620.

Dhingra, K. (2008). Towards science educational spaces as dynamic and coauthored communities of practice. *Cultural Studies of Science Education, 3*, 123–144.

Dorman, J. P. (2014). Classroom psychosocial environment and course experiences in pre-service teacher education courses at an Australian university. *Studies in Higher Education, 39*, 34–47.

Dryden, M., & Fraser, B. J. (1998, April). *The impact of systemic reform efforts in promoting constructivist approaches in high school science.* Paper presented at the annual meeting of the American Educational Research Association, San Diego, CA.

Ebrahimi, N. A. (2015). Validation and application of the constructivist learning environment survey in English language teacher education classrooms in Iran. *Learning Environments Research, 18*, 69–93.

Epstein, A., Easton, J., Murthy, R., Davidson, E., de Bruijn, J., Hayse, T., Hens, E., & Lloyd, M. (2010, January). *Helping engineering and science students find their voice: Radio production as a way to enhance students' communication skills and their competence at placing engineering and science in a broader societal context*. Proceedings of the American Society for Engineering Education Annual Conference. Retrieved December, 2015, from https://peer.asee.org/16230

Fraser, B. J. (1981a). *Test of science-related attitudes handbook*. Melbourne: The Australian Council for Education Research Limited.

Fraser, B. J. (1981b). Using environmental assessments to make better classrooms. *Journal of Curriculum Studies, 13*(2), 131–144.

Fraser, B. J. (1986). *Classroom environment*. London: Routledge & Kegan Paul.

Fraser, B. J. (1998). Classroom environment instruments: Development, validity and applications. *Learning Environments Research: An International Journal, 1*, 7–33.

Fraser, B. J. (2002). Learning environments research: Yesterday, today and tomorrow. In S. C. Goh & M. S. Khine (Eds.), *Studies in educational learning environments: An international perspective* (pp. 1–25). Singapore: World Scientific Publishers.

Fraser, B. J. (2007). Classroom learning environments. In S. K. Abell & N. G. Lederman (Eds.), *Handbook of research on science education* (pp. 103–124). London: Lawrence Erlbaum Associates.

Fraser, B. J. (2012). Classroom learning environments: Retrospect, context and prospect. In B. J. Fraser, K. G. Tobin, & C. J. McRobbie (Eds.), *Second international handbook of science education* (pp. 1191–1239). Dordrecht: Springer.

Fraser, B. J., Aldridge, J. M., & Adolphe, F. S. G. (2010). A cross-national study of secondary science classroom environments in Australia and Indonesia. *Research in Science Education, 40*, 551–571.

Fraser, B. J., & Butts, W. L. (1982). Relationship between perceived levels of classroom individualization and science-related attitudes. *Journal of Research in Science Teaching, 19*, 143–154.

Fraser, B. J., & Fisher, D. L. (1983). Development and validation of short forms of some instruments measuring student perceptions of actual and preferred classroom learning environment. *Science Education, 67*(1), 115–131.

Fraser, B. J., & Lee, S. U. (2015). Use of Test of Science Related Attitudes (TOSRA) in Korea: Stream differences and associations with constructivist classroom environments. In M. S. Khine (Ed.), *Attitude measurements in science education: Classic and contemporary approaches* (pp. 293–308). Charlotte, NC: Information Age Publishing.

Fraser, B. J., & Treagust, D. F. (1986). Validity and use of an instrument for assessing classroom psychosocial environment in higher education. *Higher Education, 15*, 37–57.

Goh, S. F., & Fraser, B. J. (2016). Learning environment in Singapore primary science classrooms: The ideal and the real. *Journal of Education Research, 10*(3), 231–247.

Guertin, L. (2012). Community-based research projects with podcasting in introductory-level geoscience courses. *Abstracts with Programs (Geological Society of America), 44*, 611. Retrieved from https://gsa.confex.com/gsa/2012AM/webprogram/Paper205152.html

Guertin, L. (2013). Community-based research with podcasting in introductory geoscience courses. *Council on Undergraduate Research: On the Web Vignettes, 34*, 13–16.

Harwell, S. H., Gunter, S., Montgomery, S., Shelton, C., & West, D. (2001). Technology integration and the classroom learning environment: Research for action. *Learning Environments Research, 4*, 259–286.

Hasan, A., & Fraser, B. J. (2015). Effectiveness of teaching strategies for engaging adults who experienced childhood difficulties in learning mathematics. *Learning Environments Research, 18*, 1–13.

Hillman, S. J., Zeeman, S. I., Tilburg, C. E., & List, H. E. (2016). My Attitudes Toward Science (MATS): The development of a multidimensional instrument measuring students' science attitudes. *Learning Environments Research, 19*, 203–219.

Johnson, B., & McClure, R. (2004). Validity and reliability of a shortened, revised version of the Constructivist Learning Environment Survey (CLES). *Learning Environments Research, 7*, 65–80.

Kim, H. B., Fisher, D. L., & Fraser, B. J. (1999). Assessment and investigation of constructivist science learning environments in Korea. *Research in Science and Technological Education, 17*, 239–249.

Klopfer, L. E. (1971). Individualized science: Relevance for the 1970s. *Science Education, 55*, 441–448.

Kraal, E. R., & Regensburger, M. (2013). Telescopic topics: Student-created radio podcasts in a general education planetary science class. *Abstracts with Programs (Geological Society of America), 45*, 469. Retrieved from https://gsa.confex.com/gsa/2013AM/finalprogram/abstract_230059.htm

Kwan, Y. W., & Wong, A. F. L. (2014). The constructivist classroom learning environment and its associations with critical thinking ability of secondary school students in liberal studies. *Learning Environments Research, 17*, 191–207.

Lim, C.-T. D., & Fraser, B. J. (in press). Learning environments research in English classrooms. *Learning Environments Research*.

Luan, W. S., Bakar, A. R., Mee, L. Y., & Ayub, A. F. M. (2010). CLES-ICT: A scale to measure ICT constructivist learning environments in Malaysia. *Procedia Social and Behavioral Science, 2*, 295–299.

Lucas, K. B., & Tulip, D. F. (1980, September). *Scientific literacy of high school students*. Paper presented at annual conference of Australian Science Teachers Association, Canberra.

Malan, D. J. (2007). Podcasting computer science E-1. In ACM & I. Russell (Eds.), *SIGCSE 2007: Proceedings of the 38th SIGCSE technical symposium on computer science education* (pp. 389–393). New York, NY: Association for Computing Machinery.

Maor, D., & Fraser, B. J. (1996). Use of classroom environment perceptions in evaluating inquiry-based computer assisted learning. *International Journal of Science Education, 18,* 401–421.

Martin-Dunlop, C., & Fraser, B. J. (2008). Learning environment and attitudes associated with an innovative course designed for prospective elementary teachers. *International Journal of Science and Mathematics Education, 6,* 163–190.

Murray, H. A. (1938). *Explorations in personality.* New York, NY: Oxford University Press.

Nair, C. S., & Fisher, D. L. (2001). Transition from senior secondary to higher education: A learning environment perspective. *Research in Science Education, 30,* 435–450.

National Survey of Student Engagement. (2013). *A fresh look at student engagement: Annual results 2013.* Bloomington, IN: Indiana University Center for Postsecondary Research. Retrieved December, 2015, from http://www.nsse.indiana.edu/nsse_2013_results/pdf/nsse_2013_annual_results.pdf

Nix, R. K., Fraser, B. J., & Ledbetter, C. E. (2005). Evaluating an integrated science learning environment using the constructivist learning environment survey. *Learning Environments Research, 8,* 109–133.

Ogbuehi, P. I., & Fraser, B. J. (2007). Learning environment, attitudes and conceptual development associated with innovative strategies in middle-school mathematics. *Learning Environments Research, 10,* 101–114.

Oh, P. S., & Yager, R. E. (2004). Development of constructivist science classrooms and changes in student attitudes toward science learning. *Science Education Journal, 15,* 105–113.

O'Neill, T., & Calabrese-Barton, A. (2005). Uncovering student ownership in science learning: The making of a student created mini-documentary. *School Science and Mathematics, 105,* 292–301.

Peer, J., & Fraser, B. J. (2015). Sex, grade-level and stream differences in learning environment and attitudes to science in Singapore primary schools. *Learning Environments Research, 18,* 143–161.

Peiro, M. M., & Fraser, B. J. (2009). Assessment and investigation of science learning environments in the early childhood grades. In M. Ortiz & C. Rubio (Eds.), *Educational evaluation: 21st century issues and challenges* (pp. 349–365). New York, NY: Nova Science Publishers.

President's Council of Advisors on Science and Technology. (2012). *Engage to excel: Producing one million additional college graduates with degrees in science, technology, engineering, and mathematics.* Retrieved from https://www.whitehouse.gov/sites/default/files/microsites/ostp/pcast-engage-to-excel-final_feb.pdf

Pulvers, K., & Diekhoff, G. M. (1999). The relationship between academic dishonesty and college classroom environment. *Research in Higher Education, 40,* 487–498.

Schibeci, R. A., & McGaw, B. (1981). Empirical validation of the conceptual structure of a test of science-related attitudes. *Educational and Psychological Measurement, 41*, 1195–1201.

Schriesheim, C. A., & Eisenbach, R. J. (1991). The effect of negation and polar opposite item reversals on questionnaire reliability and validity: An experimental investigation. *Educational and Psychological Measurement, 51*, 67–78.

Semken, S., & Freeman, C. B. (2008). Sense of place in the practice and assessment of place-based science teaching. *Science Education, 92*, 1042–1057.

Sirrakos Jr., G., & Fraser, B. J. (2017). A cross-national mixed method study of reality pedagogy. *Learning Environments Research, 20*, 153–174.

Sobel, D. (2004). *Place-based education: Connecting classroom and community.* Barrington, MA: Orion Society.

Spinner, H., & Fraser, B. J. (2005). Evaluation of an innovative mathematics program in terms of classroom environment, student attitudes, and conceptual development. *International Journal of Science and Mathematics Education, 3*, 267–293.

Strayer, J. F. (2012). How learning in an inverted classroom influences cooperation, innovation, and task orientation. *Learning Environments Research, 15*, 171–193.

Taylor, P. C., & Fraser, B. J. (1991, April). *Development of an instrument for assessing constructivist learning environments.* Paper presented at the annual meeting of the American Educational Research Associations, New Orleans, LA.

Teh, G. P. L., & Fraser, B. J. (1995). Development and validation of an instrument for assessing the psychosocial environment of computer-assisted learning classrooms. *Journal of Educational Computing Research, 12*(2), 177–193.

Tobin, K. (1988). Issues and trends in the teaching of science. In B. J. Fraser & K. G. Tobin (Eds.), *International handbook of science education* (pp. 129–151). Dordrecht: Kluwer.

Treagust, D. F., Duit, R., & Fraser, B. J. (1996). Research on students' preinstructional conceptions: The driving force for improving teaching and learning in science and mathematics. In D. F. Treagust, R. Duit, & B. J. Fraser (Eds.), *Improving teaching and learning in science and mathematics* (pp. 1–14). New York, NY: Teachers College Press.

Walker, S. L. (2006). Development and validation of the Test of Geography-Related Attitudes (ToGRA). *The Journal of Geography, 105*, 175–181.

Wilks, D. R. (2000). *An evaluation of classroom learning environments using critical constructivist perspectives as a referent for reform* (Unpublished doctoral thesis). Curtin University of Technology, Perth, Australia.

Wolf, S. J., & Fraser, B. J. (2008). Learning environment, attitudes and achievement among middle school science students using inquiry-based laboratory activities. *Research in Science Education, 38*, 321–341.

Wong, A. F. L., & Fraser, B. J. (1996). Environment-attitude associations in the chemistry laboratory classroom. *Research in Science and Technological Education, 14*, 91–102.

Zandvliet, D. B., & Fraser, B. J. (2005). Physical and psychosocial environments associated with networked classrooms. *Learning Environments Research, 8*, 1–17.

Zeidan, F. (2015). Constructivist learning environment among Palestinian science students. *International Journal of Science and Mathematics Education, 13*, 947–964.

CHAPTER 7

Using Classroom Environment Perceptions to Guide Teacher Professional Learning

A Mixed-Methods Case Study

> *David Henderson*
> Rossmoyne Senior High School, Perth, Australia
>
> *Melissa Loh*
> Rossmoyne Senior High School, Perth, Australia

1   Introduction

This school-based professional learning program gave teachers the opportunity to participate in an individualised program based on their own needs and the needs of the students in their classes. Such a professional learning community in which teachers work together to improve classroom practice has been shown to produce positive outcomes (McLaughlin & Talbert, 2006) in providing an alternative to external short-duration workshop-style professional learning which do not necessarily suit the needs of all individual teachers (Fullan, 2007).

Our research centred on the continued development and refinement of a program to guide high-school teachers' professional learning using the learning environment perceptions of both students and teachers at the school. The study's two objectives were (1) to assess the effectiveness of the use of the Classroom Climate Questionnaire (CCQ) and a structured Disciplined Collaboration program for facilitating teacher professional development and (2) to evaluate ways in which teacher feedback from the use of structured classroom observation could be integrated with student feedback from the use of the CCQ.

2   Perspectives

2.1   *Students' Learning Environment Perceptions*
For more than 40 years classroom learning environments have provided a particular focus for research in education (Fraser, 2014). The development

of the Learning Environment Inventory (LEI, Walberg, & Anderson, 1968) and the Classroom Environment Scale (CES, Moos, & Trickett, 1974) provided pioneering studies in which students' perceptions of their learning environment could be measured by gathering their responses to items in a questionnaire. A range of such questionnaires reviewed by Fraser (2012) now enable researchers to gather perceptions of students in varied educational environments at the primary, secondary and tertiary levels of education. These questionnaires include the Individualised Classroom Environment Questionnaire (ICEQ, Fraser, 1982; Fraser & Butts, 1982), Questionnaire on Teacher Interaction (QTI, Goh, & Fraser, 2000; Wubbels & Levy, 1993) and Technology-Rich Outcomes-Focused Learning Environment Inventory (TROFLEI, Aldridge, & Fraser, 2008).

Fraser (2012) outlined 11 ways in which learning environment instruments have been used in past research, such as evaluations of educational programs (Spinner & Fraser, 2005). One particular research focus has been the use of 'actual' and 'preferred' versions of a questionnaire to compare students' perceptions of the environment currently experienced with their perceptions of the environment they would ideally like or prefer (Byrne, Hattie, & Fraser, 1986; Fraser & Fisher, 1983c). Such a comparison is based on the concept of person–environment fit, which is defined as the degree to which individual and environmental characteristics match (Dawis, 1992). Fraser and Fisher's (1983a, 1983b) research indicated that students' achievement could be enhanced if their actual learning environment is altered to more closely match their preferred learning environment, and Edwards and Shipp (2007) suggest that a closely-aligned person–environment fit leads to positive outcomes, such as satisfaction, commitment, performance and reduced stress.

Fraser (1991) proposed how teachers could use students' actual and preferred perceptions to bring about changes aimed at improving their classroom learning environment. The five-step procedure in this model includes: *assessment* of students' perceptions on actual and preferred forms of a learning environment instrument; *feedback* to teachers involving a graphical representation of mean actual and preferred scores of each scale; *reflection and discussion* by teachers about discrepancies between actual and preferred scores and a decision about whether to change a selected dimension (or dimensions); *intervention* by the teacher over a period of about two months in an attempt to change the classroom environment; *reassessment* of actual environment at the end of the intervention period to determine whether students perceive their environment differently from before (Fraser & Aldridge, 2017). This model has been extensively used over the past three decades in a considerable number of attempts by teachers to improve their classroom environments and using a variety of learning environment instruments (Aldridge, Fraser, & Sebela, 2004; Yarrow, Millwater, & Fraser, 1997).

2.2 *Classroom Observations*

Classroom observations by a teacher's colleagues or by educators external to a learning institution can complement or indeed provide an alternative to the use of students' perceptions of their learning environment. Classroom observations played an integral part of the Measures of Effective Teaching (MET) project (Kane, Kerr, & Pianta, 2014), a national project for identifying and developing effective teaching in schools in the United States. A national project to promote classroom observations in schools in Australia is currently underway and includes guidelines aligned with the National Professional Standards for Teachers produced by the Australian Institute for Teaching and School Leadership (AITSL, 2011). In Western Australia, classroom observation has been mandated by the local education authority (Department of Education, Western Australia, 2015).

3 Methods

In 2012, teachers at an independent public high school in Western Australia were invited to participate in a professional learning program involving use of the Classroom Climate Questionnaire (CCQ, Aldridge, Fraser, Bell, & Dorman, 2012), which can be used to gather high-school students' actual and preferred perceptions of their learning environment in any subject discipline. The professional learning program followed the above five-step intervention process that teachers can use in their attempts to increase the congruence between their students' actual and preferred perceptions, as adopted in many professional learning programs (e.g., Bell & Aldridge, 2014; Fraser & Aldridge, 2017).

During the development of this professional learning program, it was considered essential that the learning environment instrument selected could be used in any high school classroom regardless of subject discipline. Other generic instruments, including the Questionnaire on Teacher Interaction (QTI, Wubbels, & Levy, 1993) and the What Is Happening in This Class? (WIHIC, Fraser, Fisher, & McRobbie, 1996) were considered for use in this professional learning program, but the CCQ was preferred because of the timely, comprehensive and easily interpreted report available to participating teachers.

The development, validation and use of the CCQ are detailed by Aldridge, Fraser, Bell, and Dorman (2012). The instrument comprises 66 items grouped into 11 scales, and there are 'actual' and 'preferred' forms of each item. Whereas the 'actual' form measures students' perceptions of their actual or experienced learning environment, the preferred form measures students' perceptions of the environment ideally liked or preferred. The 11 scales of the CCQ are: Student Cohesiveness; Teacher Support; Equity; Young Adult Ethos; Formative Assessment; Clarity of Assessment; Differentiation; Task Orientation; Involvement; Personal Relevance; and Cooperation.

Table 7.1 outlines the focus of each CCQ dimension and groups the scales into Relationships, Assessment and Delivery dimensions (Bell & Aldridge, 2014).

TABLE 7.1 CCQ scales and their allocation to three dimensions (adapted from Bell & Aldridge, 2014)

Dimension	Focus of dimension	CCQ scales allocated to dimension
Relationships	The group dynamics in the classroom	Student Cohesiveness; Teacher Support; Equity; Young Adult Ethos
Assessment	The assessment practices used in the course	Formative Assessment; Clarity of Assessment
Delivery	The ways that learning is organised in the classroom	Differentiation; Task Orientation; Involvement; Personal Relevance; Cooperation

Students respond to each CCQ item on a five-point frequency scale with the responses Almost Never, Rarely, Sometimes, Often and Almost Always.

Following its success in 2012, the CCQ-based professional learning program was continued at the high school in 2013 and 2014, when teachers were also invited to participate in a national Disciplined Collaboration (DC) program initiated and coordinated by the Australian Institute for Teaching and School Leadership (AITSL, 2014). The aim of Disciplined Collaboration is to create professional learning communities (DuFour, 2004; Little, Gearhart, Curry, & Kafka, 2003) in which teachers work in an authentic and interdependent way with sustained engagement and a particular focus (Harris & Jones, 2010). The purpose of the Disciplined Collaboration program at the high school was to enable teachers to share in a more structured way their ideas and experiences regarding the intervention strategies that they were using as part of their involvement in the CCQ program (Henderson & Loh, 2015).

USING CLASSROOM ENVIRONMENT PERCEPTIONS TO GUIDE TEACHER   131

Following a trial in late 2014, the high school introduced a Classroom Observation program in 2015 in line with the requirements of the Department of Education of Western Australia (2015). The classroom observations were to be based on the recommendations of the Professional Practice Domain of the Australian Professional Standards for Teachers (AITSL, 2011). The steps in the 2015 professional learning program were:

1. Each teacher who had volunteered to be involved selected a class considered appropriate for his/her study.
2. Teachers administered an electronic form of the actual and preferred versions of the CCQ to the students in their selected class.
3. As soon as students had completed responding to the CCQ, their teacher was able to download a comprehensive report on his/her students' responses (see Figure 7.1). Teachers had the option of sharing the details of their report with their peers if they wished.
4. Each teacher selected one scale of the CCQ for which there was a clear disparity between students' actual and preferred perceptions and for which the teacher felt that he/she would be able to make changes to the actual learning environment as measured by the items in this scale.
5. Once teachers had selected the scale as the focus for their intervention, this information was added to a database in order to enable teachers who

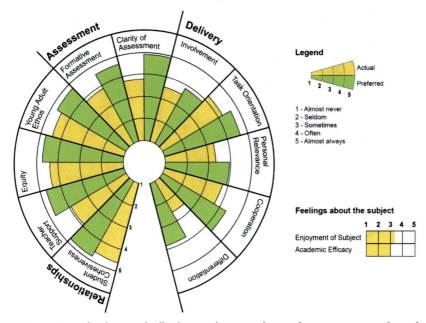

FIGURE 7.1   Example of pretest feedback to teachers regarding students' perceptions of actual and preferred learning environment

were addressing the same scale to meet and discuss their intervention strategies as part of the school's Disciplined Collaboration program.
6. Teachers who had decided on a scale as the focus for their intervention strategies were invited to participate in the Classroom Observation program which involved a classroom visit from two teachers who were involved in using the CCQ and who focussed their observations on the

Average response for specific items for this scale			
Item		1 2 3	
7.	The teacher considers my feelings.	Actual	4.21
		Preferred	4.79
8.	The teacher helps me when I have trouble with the work.	Actual	4.07
		Preferred	4.86
9.	The teacher talks with me.	Actual	3.86
		Preferred	4.71
10.	The teacher takes an interest in my progress.	Actual	4.07
		Preferred	4.93
11.	The teacher moves about the class to talk with me.	Actual	3.57
		Preferred	4.50

FIGURE 7.2   Extract from pretest report showing items means for teacher support scale

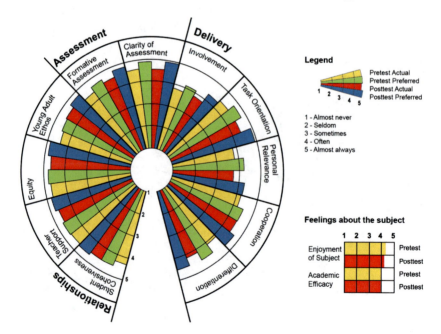

FIGURE 7.3   Example of pretest and posttest feedback to teachers regarding students' perceptions of actual and preferred learning environment

chosen scale. Each teacher received detailed written and verbal feedback following such a visit. Once the teacher had decided on the scale to be used for intervention, details in the pretest report could be used to help the teacher focus on particular aspects of the scale. For example, Figure 7.2 shows that Items 11 and 12 could provide a particular focus for intervention strategies bearing in mind not only the disparity between actual and preferred scores, but also the relatively low pretest scores.

7. After an intervention period of 4–6 weeks, each teacher administered the actual and preferred versions of the CCQ to the same class as a posttest. Only students who completed the pretest were invited to complete the posttest.
8. Examination of a detailed report based on students' responses to the posttest enabled teachers to judge the effectiveness of their intervention strategies.

3.1   Classroom Observation Program

The development and implementation of this school's professional learning program was strongly influenced by the concept of Visible Teaching and Learning which "occurs when there is deliberate practice aimed at attaining mastery of the goal, when there is feedback given and sought and where there are active, passionate and engaging people (students, teachers, peers) participating in the act of learning" (Hattie, 2012, p. 12). The addition of the Classroom Observation program now enables teachers to receive feedback from their peers, to complement that received from their students' responses to the pretest CCQ. For a teacher whose class has already completed the pretest CCQ and who has identified the focus scale, the steps in the Classroom Observation program are as follows:

1. The Observer and the teacher meet to clarify the focus scale and to ensure that the teacher has an understanding of the process.
2. The Observer enters the classroom at the pre-arranged time and is free to walk around the classroom to interact with the teacher and students.
3. The Observer takes notes on any strengths, weaknesses and suggested improvements in skills and techniques related to the focus scale.
4. The Observer and teacher meet at a later time meet to discuss strategies which could be put in place to improve the teacher's focus construct.
5. Over a 4–6 week period, the participant works towards improving aspects of the focus construct using the qualitative feedback provided through classroom observations as well as reflection on CCQ pretest results.
6. The teacher's students complete their posttest CCQ and a report is subsequently generated to enable the teacher to judge the effectiveness of the intervention strategies (see Figure 7.3).
7. The Observer discusses, supports and reflects on these results with the teacher.

Through the use of this convergent parallel mixed-methods approach (Creswell, 2013), the *teacher is able to merge quantitative data from the pretest* CCQ *and qualitative data from* classroom observation to provide a more comprehensive and complete analysis of the teacher's classroom learning environment. The teacher is then able to integrate all of the information acquired and use it to inform intervention strategies that will be implemented.

4   Results

4.1   *CCQ Program*

The number of teachers who have voluntarily participated in the school's CCQ program has steadily increased from 16 teachers in 2012 to 40 teachers in 2015 – representing about 25% of the school's teaching staff. The sample of teachers has a disproportionate number of females (70%, with only 51% of the school's teachers being female), early-career teachers and teachers in non-promotable positions. The results for the 2014 program are summarised below.

Examination of all teachers' final reports revealed that, for the scale chosen by the teacher as the focus for their intervention strategies, students' perceptions of their actual learning environment on the posttest questionnaire more closely matched their preferred perceptions on the pretest questionnaire. Some of the changes were quite small, but this was especially evident in some classes where students' pretest perceptions were rated as 'Often' (numerically between 4 and 5) and therefore there was little opportunity for further optimising the learning environment.

Teachers' efforts to improve one aspect of their classroom were often associated with positive changes in students' perceptions on other CCQ scales. Apparently, some of the skills, techniques and strategies used to change, further define and improve identified scales also positively affected students' perceptions on some of the other scales as evidenced by increased congruence between students' actual and preferred perceptions on the posttest CCQ.

The reactions of all teachers to the evidence that their intervention strategies were associated with more favourable student perceptions were very positive. The fact that teachers perceived that they could make such changes helped them to feel more in control of their classroom environments and to realise that they were able to improve students' learning outcomes by undertaking such a program of professional learning. Comments from teachers suggested that this is an important reason for the growing participation of teachers in the CCQ program.

When pretest and posttest data for the whole school in 2014 were considered with regard to student gender, noticeable differences were seen. For female students (n=222), changes in the learning environment between pretest and posttest were positive for 10 of the 11 scales (with one showing no change) whereas, for male students (n=165), only two scales were rated more positively at posttesting.

When whole-school data were analysed according to year group, pretest-posttest differences for the CCQ were evident for the three year groups (8, 9 and 10) for which more than three classes were involved. Improvements in CCQ perceptions between pretest and posttest were larger for Year 9 classes (n=95 students) than for Year 10 students (n=145) or Year 11students (n=99). Whilst teachers are free to select any class, teachers new to the program are made aware of these findings and encouraged to select a Year 9 class where possible. Teachers also are counselled against using Year 11 or Year 12 classes because of the disruption to the timetable associated with school-based examinations during the year.

4.2 *Disciplined Collaboration Program*

The Disciplined Collaboration program brought together staff members from different Learning Areas. This opportunity to meet and focus on improvements in pedagogy rather than on subject content allowed individual staff members to feel more supported by their peers in increasing communication outside their Learning Area, gaining insight into other teachers' expertise, and becoming more open to and acknowledging colleagues' different perspectives. As more teachers have become involved in the CCQ program over the past four years, it became increasingly difficult to organise meeting times suitable for all teachers wishing to participate. The compilation of a database listing the scale addressed by each participating teacher provided an alternative, but this lacked the rigour and focus of the whole-group meetings of previous years. The inclusion of the Classroom Observation program was seen as a means of addressing this issue. Below are some of the comments from teachers about what they learned when reflecting on their involvement in Disciplined Collaboration meetings:

- Some good ideas that can be shared with other teachers to enhance their teaching;
- Ways to explicitly teach study skills to enable students to take responsibility for their own learning;
- More about collaborative learning strategies;
- More about assessment strategies;
- Reflection leading to improvement;
- Becoming an active listener;
- Ways of sharing ideas with others;

- Having an optimal classroom environment requires consultation with others;
- New strategies for creating a passion for learning among students;
- New strategies to encourage autonomous learning.

4.3 Classroom Observation Program

Remarks from teachers following classroom observations were highly most positive, including:
- The feedback from the visiting teachers gave me another viewpoint on my focus scale.
- I felt a real sense of collegiality with the visiting teacher when working towards a similar goal.
- It is good to receive feedback from fellow teachers, including ideas not related to my focus scale.
- I feel more comfortable receiving feedback from other classroom teachers than from senior staff.
- I gained emotional support by being able to share and reflect on situations for which I had felt frustrated in the classroom.

5 Relevance and Significance

The continued growth in high-school teachers' participation in the CCQ-based professional learning program is testament to its efficacy in providing easily-accessible data that can direct teachers' efforts to improve their classroom learning environments. The whole-school data can be used by teachers when planning their participation in the program. Teachers' responses to the provision of qualitative data from teacher classroom visits in the early stages of this program suggest that the two data sources indeed are complementary, giving a richer guidance to teachers' attempts to change their learning environments. The inclusion of teacher observers inevitably involved a greater proportion of the school's teaching staff, further diversifying the support given to teachers in their efforts to improve the learning environments of their students. Teachers' invariably-positive comments about their involvement in the program include:
- Structured and easily-interpreted feedback on my teaching practice
- Privacy of the information – no need to share with others if I didn't wish to
- Non-threatening nature of survey
- Allowing student voices to be heard
- Making me more aware of students' perspectives

– Often challenging to my perceptions about the classroom environment
– Simply the most effective PL ever.

The school's approach to teacher professional learning through this program is consistent with some key aspects of the national Grattan Report (Goss & Sonneman, 2017):

1.1 Classroom environments affect teachers and students.
5.1 School-wide approaches are critical.
5.2.2 Teachers collaborating with colleagues is important.
5.2.3 Providing teachers with tools for assessing and improving their approaches to engaging students is important.
6.2.1 Investing in tools at scale to help teachers improve practice is important.
6.2.1 Student feedback is valuable.

Teachers' continuing involvement in the program is now a system priority of this high school. It was a key strategy in the school's Business Plan for 2013–2016 and continues to be a focus in the 2017–2020 Business Plan (Anon, 2017).

6   Concluding Remarks

The success of this professional learning program is reflected in the continued increase in the number of teachers participating in the program and its integration into the school's culture and future planning. Features of the program that underlie its appeal to teachers include its focus on day-to-day teaching, the presentation of student feedback in an easily-accessible form, clear guidance from peers in the development and implementation of intervention strategies, and the use of teacher observations to supplement questionnaire feedback from students.

References

Aldridge, J. M., & Fraser, B. J. (2008). *Outcomes-focused learning environments: Determinants and effects* (Advances in Learning Environments Research Series). Rotterdam, The Netherlands: Sense Publishers.

Aldridge, J. M., Fraser, B. J., Bell, L., & Dorman, J. P. (2012). Using a new learning environment questionnaire for reflection in teacher action research. *Journal of Science Teacher Education, 23*, 259–290.

Aldridge, J. M., Fraser, B. J., & Sebela, M. P. (2004). Using teacher action research to promote constructivist learning environments in South Africa. *South African Journal of Education, 24*(4), 245–253.

Anon. (2017). *Business plan, 2017–2020: Preparing future ready citizens.* Perth: Rossmoyne Senior High School.

Australian Institute for Teaching and School Leadership (AITSL). (2011). *National professional standards for teachers.* Melbourne: Australian Institute for Teaching and School Leadership.

Australian Institute for Teaching and School Leadership (AITSL). (2014). *Disciplined collaboration in professional learning.* Melbourne: Australian Institute for Teaching and School Leadership.

Bell, L. M., & Aldridge, J. M. (2014). *Student voice, teacher action research and classroom improvement.* Rotterdam, The Netherlands: Sense Publishers.

Byrne, D. B., Hattie, J. A., & Fraser, B. J. (1986). Student perceptions of preferred classroom learning environment. *The Journal of Educational Research, 80*(1), 10–18.

Creswell, J. W. (2013). *Research design: Qualitative, quantitative and mixed methods approaches* (4th ed.). Thousand Oaks, CA: Sage Publications.

Dawis, R. V. (1992). The individual differences tradition in counseling psychology. *Journal of Counseling Psychology, 39,* 7–19.

Department of Education, Western Australia. (2015). *Focus 2015: Directions for schools.* Perth: The Government of Western Australia.

DuFour, R. (2004). What is a "professional learning community"? *Educational Leadership, 61*(8), 6–11.

Edwards, J. R., & Shipp, A. J. (2007). The relationship between person-environment fit and outcomes: An interactive theoretical framework. In C. Ostroff & T. A. Judge (Eds.), *Perspective on organizational fit* (pp. 209–258). San Francisco, CA: Jossey-Bass.

Fraser, B. J. (1981). Using environmental assessments to make better classrooms. *Journal of Curriculum Studies, 13,* 131–144.

Fraser, B. J. (1982). Individualized classroom environment questionnaire. *American Journal of Evaluation, 3*(2), 72–73.

Fraser, B. J. (2012). Classroom learning environments: Retrospect, context and prospect. In B. J. Fraser, K. G. Tobin, & C. J. McRobbie (Eds.), *Second international handbook of science education* (pp. 1191–1239). New York, NY: Springer.

Fraser, B. J. (2014). Classroom learning environments: Historical and contemporary perspectives. In N. G. Lederman & S. K. Abell (Eds.), *Handbook of research on science education* (Vol. 2, pp. 104–119). New York, NY: Routledge.

Fraser, B. J., & Aldridge, J. M. (2017). Improving classrooms through assessment of learning environments. In J. P. Bakken (Ed.), *Classrooms: Assessment practices for teachers and student improvement strategies* (pp. 91–107). New York, NY: Nova Science.

Fraser, B. J., & Butts, W. L. (1982). Relationship between perceived levels of classroom individualization and science-related attitudes. *Journal of Research in Science Teaching, 19*(2), 143–154.

Fraser, B. J., & Fisher, D. L. (1983a). Student achievement as a function of person-environment fit: A regression surface analysis. *British Journal of Educational Psychology, 53*, 89–99.

Fraser, B. J., & Fisher, D. L. (1983b). Use of actual and preferred classroom environment scales in person-environment fit research. *Journal of Educational Psychology, 75*, 303–313.

Fraser, B. J., & Fisher, D. L. (1983c). Development and validation of short forms of some instruments measuring student perceptions of actual and preferred classroom learning environment. *Science Education, 67*(1), 115–131.

Fraser, B. J., & Fisher, D. L. (1986). Using short forms of classroom climate instruments to assess and improve classroom psychosocial environment. *Journal of Research in Science Teaching, 5*, 387–413.

Fraser, B. J., Fisher, D. L., & McRobbie, C. J. (1996, April). *Development, validation and use of personal and class forms of a new classroom environment instrument.* Paper presented at the Annual Meeting of the American Educational Research Association, New York.

Fullan, M. (2007). *The new meaning of educational change* (4th ed.). New York, NY: Teachers College Press.

Goh, S. C., & Fraser, B. J. (2000). Teacher interpersonal behavior and elementary students' outcomes. *Journal of Research in Childhood Education, 14*(2), 216–231.

Goss, P., & Sonnemann, J. (2017, February). *Engaging students: Creating classrooms that improve learning.* Melbourne: Grattan Institute.

Harris, A., & Jones, M. (2010). Professional learning communities and system improvement. *Improving Schools, 13*(2), 172–181.

Hattie, J. (2012). *Visible learning for teachers: Maximizing impact on learning.* London: Routledge.

Henderson, D., & Loh, M. (2015, April). *Using students' perceptions of their learning environment to create a professional learning community.* Paper presented at the Annual Meeting of the American Educational Research Association, Chicago, IL.

Kane, T. J. Kerr, K. A., & Pianta, R. C. (2014). *Teacher evaluation systems: New guidance from the measures of effective teaching project.* San Francisco, CA: Jossey-Bass.

Little, J. W., Gearhart, M., Curry, M., & Kafka, J. (2003). Looking at student work for teacher learning, teacher community, and school reform. *Phi Delta Kappan, 83*(5), 184–192.

McLaughlin, M. W., & Talbert, J. E. (2006). *Building school-based teacher learning communities: Professional strategies to improve student achievement.* New York, NY: Teachers College Press.

Moos, R. H., & Trickett, E. J. (1974). *Classroom climate scale manual.* Palo Alto, CA: Consulting Psychologists Press.

Spinner, H., & Fraser, B. J. (2005). Evaluation of an innovative mathematics program in terms of classroom environment, student attitudes and conceptual development. *International Journal of Science and Mathematics Education, 3*(2), 267–293.

Walberg, H. J., & Anderson, G. J. (1968). Classroom climate and individual learning. *Journal of Educational Psychology, 59,* 414–419.

Wubbels, Th., & Levy, J. (Eds.). (1993). *Do you know what you look like? Interpersonal relationships in education.* London: Falmer Press.

Yarrow, A., Millwater, J., & Fraser, B. J. (1997). Improving university and primary school classroom environments through preservice teachers' action research. *International Journal of Practical Experiences in Professional Education, 1,* 68–93.

CHAPTER 8

Impacts of Learning Environments on Student Well-Being in Higher Education

Alisa Stanton
Simon Fraser University, Burnaby, Canada

David B. Zandvliet
Simon Fraser University, Burnaby, Canada

Rosie Dhaliwal
Simon Fraser University, Burnaby, Canada

1 Background and Rationale

Over the past several decades, there has been considerable interest in defining and measuring learning environments and investigating their effects on student, teacher and educational outcomes (Fraser, 1986, 1994, 2012; Fraser & Walberg, 1991; Taylor, Fraser, & Fisher, 1997). This research has taken place in elementary-, secondary- and higher-education settings and has demonstrated that various psychosocial and physical aspects of the learning environment can have important impacts on both cognitive and affective outcomes including student satisfaction with learning, academic achievement and self-esteem (Cohen et al., 2009; Fraser & Butts, 1982; McRobbie & Fraser, 1993; Walberg, 1969; Zandvliet & Fraser, 2005). These include dimensions such as student cohesiveness, teacher support, involvement and integration (Fraser, 2012; Fraser, Treagust, & Dennis, 1986). Studies exploring person–environment fit have also demonstrated that the positive impacts on student outcomes are enhanced when there is greater congruence between the actual learning environment and those preferred by students (Fraser & Fisher, 1983).

Some of the most widely-utilised learning environment tools, along with the constructs that they measure, are outlined below (Aldridge & Fraser, 2008; Fraser, 2014):
– What Is Happening In this Class? (WIHIC) – Student Cohesiveness, Teacher Support, Involvement, Investigation, Task Orientation, Cooperation and Equity

- Constructivist Learning Environment Survey (CLES) – Personal Relevance, Uncertainty, Critical Voice, Shared Control and Student Negotiation
- Science Laboratory Environment Inventory (SLEI) – Student Cohesiveness, Open-Endedness, Integration, Rule Clarity and Material Environment

Preferred forms (Byrne, Hattie, & Fraser, 1986) and short forms (Fraser & Fisher, 1983) of learning environment instruments have facilitated the widespread use of these questionnaires in evaluations of innovations (Spinner & Fraser, 2005), school psychology (Burden & Fraser, 1993) and teachers' action research aimed at improving their classrooms (Fraser, 1981).

Although extensive research has demonstrated the links between classroom learning environments and a wide range of student outcomes (Fraser, 2012), there is an important opportunity to apply learning environments research methods in exploring the impacts of learning environments on student well-being more specifically. Some recent studies have begun to explore these issues in relation to human flourishing and other theoretical foundations from positive psychology (Awartani, Whitman, & Gordon, 2008; Waxman, Rivera, Linn, Padron, Rollins, Boriack, & Alford, 2016). In particular, Waxman et al. (2016) developed a tool to measure five elements of a flourishing classroom and the corresponding impacts on student well-being, namely, (a) positive emotion (b) engagement (c) meaning (d) positive relationships and (e) accomplishment. These elements are based in Seligman's (2011) theories of well-being. In contrast, Awartani et al. (2008) outlined nine domains of well-being that could be impacted by the learning environment and emphasised the importance of student voice in the design of learning experiences.

Other studies, that have not specifically referenced learning environments literature, have documented the impacts of school climate on student outcomes related to learning, self-esteem and sense of belonging (Bear, Gaskins, Blank, & Chen, 2011; Waters, Cross, & Runions, 2009; Way, Reddy, & Rhodes, 2007). Many of these studies have reinforced the importance of teacher–student interactions and opportunities for student involvement. In particular, research from the application of Self-Determination Theory within teaching and learning settings has shown that teachers' efforts to support students' experiences of autonomy, relatedness and competence have beneficial and lasting impacts on student learning and well-being (Niemiec & Ryan, 2009).

Because students spend a large proportion of their time at school (Fraser, 2012), the learning environment is a very important setting for exploring and understanding student well-being. As the literature on human flourishing and well-being evolves, it will be important to develop tools to measure the impacts of learning environments on these important student outcomes. Our research is timely and relevant given the recent release of a new International Charter on Health Promoting Universities (Okanagan Charter, 2015), that calls on universities and colleges to design and deliver their academic programs in ways that support and enhance student well-being. Not only are student isolation, distress and depression on the rise within higher education institutions, but these experiences are known to be determinants of negative outcomes related to learning and personal well-being (Cohen, 2006; Herrman, Saxena, & Moodie, 2005). A recent survey of over 42,000 higher-education students in Canada reported that, whereas 68% of students had felt isolated at some point in the last 12 months, 52% had experienced overwhelming anxiety (American College Health Association, 2016). Similar trends in both the United States and Europe (ACHA, 2017; Royal College of Psychiatrists, 2011) highlight increasing challenges related to university students' mental well-being. These findings are concerning and have prompted higher-education institutions to focus attention and resources on creating higher education learning environments that support student well-being.

2 Methods

The purpose of this study was to explore the impacts of learning environments on student well-being within a higher-education setting. Several psychosocial scales from the WIHIC and also the Place-based Learning and Constructivist Environment Survey (PLACES, Zandvliet, 2012) were adapted for use in our questionnaire. To these, we added measures of well-being, including the PANAS affective well-being scale (Crawford & Henry, 2004), the Flourishing Scale (Diener, Wirtz, Tov, Kim-Prieto, Oishi, & Biswas-Diener, 2009) and a single item measuring of Life Satisfaction (Cheung & Lucas, 2014).

The surveys were administered to 842 undergraduate students in 13 classes. The sample was selected by the Simon Fraser University (SFU) Office of Institutional Research and Planning and included a range of class levels (i.e. first, second, third and fourth year courses), as well as a range of faculties and class sizes. This was intentional to ensure that variability within the sample would be high. This is important because the largest effect sizes in terms of impact on well-being are likely to occur when the variance in learning environment variables is large. The faculties represented in the sample included Health Sciences, Science & Arts and Social Sciences. The survey was administered anonymously in pen-and-pencil format. Student demographic information was not collected. All responses were self-reported by students, because this has been shown to be an effective and accurate way to record learning environment variables (Fraser, Treagust, & Dennis, 1986). For each item, students responded on a five-point scale ranging from strongly disagree to strongly agree. Ethics approval was granted by the SFU Office of Research Ethics, and a response rate of approximately 70% was obtained.

The reliability of the adapted survey was estimated using Cronbach's alpha coefficient for the internal consistency of each scale. Following this process, several survey items were removed. The remaining items were used to explore correlations between learning environment conditions (measured by the WIHIC, PLACES and well-being scales). In particular, life satisfaction was used as the primary dependent variable because it has been shown to be an effective single-item measure of overall well-being that shows strong consistency with other measures of well-being (Cheung & Lucas, 2014). The independent variable was a single composite of the learning environment scales. More specifically, the 13 classes were categorised as having learning environments that were positive, neutral or negative based on the overall average of student responses to learning environment items for that class. These three learning environment groupings were then analysed in terms of their associations with life satisfaction outcomes using a one-way ANOVA. We were able to identify whether students experienced any differences in life satisfaction according to whether they were in classes that were rated as positive, neutral or negative in terms of the overall learning environment.

This exploratory method of analysis enabled us to build on of existing methods used in learning environments research while taking into consideration important theoretical understandings from public and population health research. In particular, the WIHIC and PLACES provided important validated scales with which aspects of the psychosocial learning environment could be assessed in order to determine their association with well-being. Although most learning environments research is analysed at the class level, population health impacts are best measured by taking well-being measures at the individual level and comparing outcomes on these variables by treatment groups within the population. In this case, we could not determine the treatment group ahead of time because we could not predict how students would experience the learning environment in each class. The treatment groups were therefore determined after the fact and based on students' reports of the learning environment within each class. As described above, these reports enabled the classes to be grouped into three learning environment groups (positive, neutral or negative) whose life satisfaction ratings could then be compared.

3 Analyses and Results

The distribution of the dependent variable of life satisfaction was approximately normal. The descriptive statistics reported in Table 8.1 show that the data for the dependent variable (life satisfaction) were spread across the three learning environment groups of the independent variable (rated as positive, neutral or negative). The life satisfaction mean for the positive (high-scoring) environment group (7.57) was higher than that for the neutral group (6.92), which in turn was higher than that for the negative group (6.66). ANOVA provides an assessment of whether these differences between environment were statistically significant. The overall life satisfaction standard deviation of 1.866 varied between the three learning environment groups.

TABLE 8.1 Descriptive statistics for the life satisfaction variable for three learning environment groups

Learning environment group	N	Mean	SD	Std. error	95% Confidence interval for mean Lower bound	95% Confidence interval for mean Upper bound	Minimum	Maximum
Negative	216	6.66	1.966	0.134	6.39	6.92	0	10
Neutral	197	6.92	1.860	0.132	6.66	7.19	0	10
Positive	49	7.57	1.137	0.162	7.24	7.90	5	10
Total	462	6.87	1.866	0.087	6.70	7.04	0	10

A one-way ANOVA was used to investigate differences between the three learning environment groups (positive, neutral or negative) in their ratings of student life satisfaction. Because Levene's test suggested that ANOVA's homogeneity of variance assumption had been violated, the Welch test was used to ascertain statistical significance. ANOVA results in Table 8.2 indicate that there was a statistically-significant difference between the three learning environment groups on the dependent variable of life satisfaction.

In order to determine which pairs of learning environment groups were significantly different from each other in life satisfaction, the Games-Howell post hoc test was used because it is appropriate when there is heterogeneity of variance among groups. The results in Table 8.3 indicate that a statistically-

TABLE 8.2 ANOVA results for differences among three learning environment groups in ratings of life satisfaction

Source	Sum of squares	Df	Mean square	F	p
Between groups	34.440	2	17.220	5.033	0.007
Within groups	1570.506	459	3.422		
Total	1604.946	461			

significant difference ($p < 0.05$) occurred between the negative and positive groups and between the neutral and positive groups, but not between the negative rated and neutral groups.

TABLE 8.3 Games-Howell post hoc test for multiple comparisons of life satisfaction across three learning environment groupings

Pairwise comparison of learning environment groups	Mean difference	Std. error	p	95% Confidence interval Lower bound	95% Confidence interval Upper bound
Negative vs. Neutral	−0.266	0.188	0.334	−0.71	0.18
Negative vs. Positive	−0.914*	0.210	0.000	−1.41	−0.41
Neutral vs. Positive	−0.648*	0.210	0.007	−1.14	−0.15

* The mean difference is significant at the 0.05 level.

4   Discussion and Limitations

One-way ANOVA revealed a significant difference between three groups of students with different perceptions of their learning environments (rated as positive, neutral or negative based on scores from WIHIC and PLACES scales) in terms of their overall well-being (as measured by self-reported life satisfaction). In particular, students who reported experiencing positive learning environments reported significantly higher self-reported life satisfaction than those who reported experiencing either negative or neutral perceptions about the learning environment. Those who reported neutral perceptions of the learning environment also reported higher life satisfaction than those who reported negative perceptions on the learning environment, but this difference was not statistically significant. These findings are important because they indicate that, as students' experiences of conditions within the learning environment become more positive, so too do their self-reports of life satisfaction. This provides initial evidence that a relationship could exist between students' experiences of learning environments and students' well-being outcomes. Such a relationship would provide evidence of the importance of providing instructors with skills and resources to support them in creating learning environments that are conducive to student well-being as a means of enhancing and supporting well-being in higher-education settings. Because students in higher education are reported as experiencing negative well-being outcomes at increasingly-high levels (American College Health Association, 2016), it is important to consider whether creating positive conditions for well-being in postsecondary learning environments could provide an avenue for supporting student well-being more broadly within and across higher-education institutions. This is particularly important given the recent international interest in adopting a healthy-settings approach within colleges and universities (Okanagan Charter, 2015) that emphasises the importance of designing academic programs and policies in ways that enhance and support student health and well-being.

These results must be interpreted with caution because there were several limitations to the study. Firstly, because both the outcome variable and independent variable were self-reported measures, there could be bias in students' reporting that affects the results. For example, students who tend to report their experiences in learning environments more favourably also might report their life satisfaction more favourably, thus inflating the apparent associations between these variables. Secondly, because space restrictions on the survey did not allow collection of student demographic information, it was not possible to confirm the representativeness of the sample. However, because the response rate was fairly high at approximately 70%, the chances that response bias had a large impact on the results was minimised. Finally, the direction of the association was assumed to be that learning experiences were having a positive impact on student well-being, but it is possible that the direction of the relationship is in fact reversed. For example, students with a higher sense of life satisfaction might be inclined to rate their learning experiences more favourably. To further understand the strength and direction of the relationship found, it is important to carry out further studies that are experimental in design to enable more-accurate understanding of cause and effect.

References

Aldridge, J. M., & Fraser, B. J. (2008). *Outcomes-focused learning environments: Determinants and effects* (Advances in Learning Environments Research Series). Rotterdam, The Netherlands: Sense Publishers.

American College Health Association (ACHA). (2016). *National college health assessment II: Canadian reference group report fall 2016*. Linthicum, MD: American College Health Association.

American College Health Association (ACHA). (2017). *National college health assessment II: Reference group executive summary spring 2017*. Linthicum, MD: American College Health Association.

Awartani, M., Whitman, C. V., & Gordon, J. (2008). Developing instruments to capture young people's perceptions of how school as a learning environment affects of their well-being. *European Journal of Education, 43*(1), 51–70.

Bear, G. G., Gaskins, C., Blank, J., & Chen, F. F. (2011). Delaware school climate survey – student: Its factor structure, concurrent validity, and reliability. *Journal of School Psychology, 49*, 157–174.

Bear, G. G., Yang, C., Pell, M., & Gaskins, C. (2014). Validation of a brief measure of teachers' perceptions of school climate: Relations to student achievement and suspensions. *Learning Environments Research, 17*, 339–354.

Burden, R. L., & Fraser, B. J. (1993). Use of classroom environment assessments in school psychology: A British perspective. *Psychology in the Schools, 30*(3), 232–240.

Byrne, D. B., Hattie, J. A., & Fraser, B. J. (1986). Student perceptions of preferred classroom learning environment. *Journal of Educational Research, 80*(1), 10–18.

Cheung, F., & Lucas, R. E. (2014). Assessing the validity of single-item life satisfaction measures: Results from three large samples. *Quality of Life Research, 23*(10), 2809–2818.

Cohen, J. (2006). Social, emotional, ethical and academic education: Creating a climate for learning, participation in democracy and well-being. *Harvard Educational Review, 76*(2), 201–237.

Cohen, J., McCabe, L., Michelli, N. M., & Pickeral, T. (2009). School climate: Research, policy, practice, and teacher education. *Teachers College Record, 111*, 180–213.

Crawford, J. R., & Henry, J. D. (2004). The Positive And Negative Affect Schedule (PANAS): Construct validity, measurement properties and normative data in a large non-clinical sample. *British Journal of Clinical Psychology, 43*(3), 245–265.

Diener, E., Wirtz, D., Tov, W., Kim-Prieto, C., Oishi, S., & Biswas-Diener, R. (2009). New measures of well-being: Flourishing and positive and negative feelings. *Social Indicators Research, 39*, 247–266.

Fraser, B. J. (1981). Using environmental assessments to make better classrooms. *Journal of Curriculum Studies, 13*(2), 131–144.

Fraser, B. J. (1986). *Classroom environment*. London: Croom Helm.

Fraser, B. J. (1994). Research on classroom and school climate. In D. Gabel (Ed.), *Handbook of research on science teaching and learning* (pp. 493–541). New York, NY: Macmillan.

Fraser, B. J. (2012). Classroom learning environments: Retrospect, context and prospect. In B. J. Fraser, K. G. Tobin, & C. J. McRobbie (Eds.), *Second international handbook of science education* (pp. 1191–1232). New York, NY: Springer.

Fraser, B. J. (2014). Classroom learning environments: Historical and contemporary perspectives. In N. G. Lederman & S. K. Abell (Eds.), *Handbook of research on science education, volume II* (pp. 104–119). New York, NY: Routledge.

Fraser, B. J., & Fisher, D. L. (1983). Student achievement as a function of person-environment lit: A regression surface analysis. *British Journal of Educational Psychology, 53*, 89–99.

Fraser, B. J., Treagust, D. F., & Dennis, N. C. (1986). Development of an instrument for assessing classroom psychosocial environment at universities and colleges. *Studies in Higher Education, 11*, 43–54.

Fraser, B. J., & Walberg, H. J. (1991). *Educational environments: Evaluation, antecedents and consequences*. Oxford: Pergamon Press.

Herrman, H. S., Saxena, S., & Moodie, R. (2005). *Promoting mental health: Concepts, emerging evidence, practice*. Geneva: World Health Organization Press.

McRobbie, C. J., & Fraser, B. J. (1993). Association between student outcomes and psychosocial science environments. *Journal of Educational Research, 87*, 78–85.

Niemiec, C. P., & Ryan, R. (2009). Autonomy, competence and relatedness in the classroom: Applying self-determination theory to educational practice. *Theory and Research in Education, 7*(2), 133–144.

Okanagan Charter: An International Charter for Health Promoting Universities and Colleges. (2015). Retrieved from http://internationalhealthycampuses2015.sites.olt.ubc.ca/files/2016/01/Okanagan-Charter-January13v2.pdf

Royal College of Psychiatrists. (2011). *Mental health of students in higher education*. London: Royal College of Psychiatrists.

Seligman, M. E. P. (2011). *Flourish: A visionary new understanding of happiness and wellbeing*. New York, NY: Free Press.

Spinner, H., & Fraser, B. J. (2005). Evaluation of an innovative mathematics program in terms of classroom environment, student attitudes, and conceptual development. *International Journal of Science and Mathematics Education, 3*, 267–293.

Taylor, P. C., Fraser, B. J., & Fisher, D. L. (1997). Monitoring constructivist classroom learning environments. *International Journal of Educational Research, 27*, 293–302.

Walberg, H. J. (1969). The social environment as mediator of classroom learning. *Journal of Educational Psychology, 60*, 443–448.

Waters, S., Cross, D., & Runions, K. (2009). Social and ecological structures supporting adolescent connectedness to school: A theoretical model. *Journal of School Health, 79*, 516–524.

Waxman, H. C., Rivera, H. H., Linn, B., Padron, Y., Rollins, K., Boriack, A., & Alford, B. (2016). Development of an observation instrument to measure flourishing learning environments. *Journal of Chinese Studies, 1*, 3–10.

Way, N., Reddy, R., & Rhodes, J. (2007). Students' perceptions of school climate during middle school years: Associations with trajectories of psychological and behavioral adjustment. *American Journal of Community Psychology, 40*(3–4), 194–213.

Zandvliet, D. B. (2012). Development and validation of the Place-based Learning And Constructivist Environment Survey (PLACES). *Learning Environments Research, 15*(1), 125–140.

Zandvliet, D. B., & Fraser, B. (2005). Physical and psychosocial environments associated with internet classrooms. *Learning Environment Research, 8*(1), 1–17.

Printed in the United States
By Bookmasters